The
Clear
Leader

T0243719

James Donald, PhD, is passionate about cultivating purposeful, self-aware and skilful leadership within teams and organizations. Since 2007, James has worked with leaders in numerous private and public sector organizations. He has a PhD in psychology, is a Senior Lecturer at the University of Sydney Business School and regularly appears in print, radio and TV media, discussing issues of workplace wellbeing and leadership. James is also an active researcher in positive psychology and leadership, regularly publishing his research in the world's leading research journals.

Professor Craig Hassed, OAM, has worked within the Faculty of Medicine at Monash University since 1989, as well as teaching other faculties, and coordinating mindfulness programs across Monash. In 2021, he became the founding Director of Education at the Monash Centre for Consciousness and Contemplative Studies (M3CS). Craig has authored 120 papers in peer-reviewed journals, and published 14 books and 17 book chapters. He is regularly invited to speak in Australia and overseas in health, educational, government and corporate contexts. Craig was the founding president and patron of Meditation Australia and a regular media commentator. He is co-author of the two top-ranked online mindfulness courses in the world, and in 2019 received the medal of the Order of Australia for services to medicine.

The
Clear
Leader

How to lead well in a hyper-connected world

JAMES N. DONALD, PHD

CRAIG S. HASSED, OAM

EXISLE
PUBLISHING

First published 2024

Exisle Publishing Pty Ltd
PO Box 864, Chatswood, NSW 2057, Australia
226 High Street, Dunedin, 9016, New Zealand
www.exislepublishing.com

A CiP record for this book is available from the National Library of Australia.

ISBN 978-1-922539-71-7

Designed by Bee Creative
Typeset in PT Serif, 11pt
Printed in China

This book uses paper sourced under ISO 14001 guidelines from well-managed forests
and other controlled sources.

10 9 8 7 6 5 4 3 2 1

Disclaimer
While this book is intended as a general information resource and all care has
been taken in compiling the contents, neither the authors nor the publisher and
their distributors can be held responsible for any loss, claim or action that may
arise from reliance on the information contained in this book. As each person and
situation is unique, this book should never be a substitute for the skill, knowledge
and experience of a qualified professional dealing with the specific facts and
circumstances of an individual.

Contents

Introduction

Ask yourself this question: When was I last at my very best? Picture in your mind a recent time when you felt connected, energized and clear. A time where you were in 'the zone' and doing your best work. In that moment, where was your attention? How much were you thinking about other things, worrying about the future, being distracted by prompts on your phone or trying to multitask? When we are at our best, we are fully present. We are open and connected with what is before us. And yet, so many of the ways we work (and are required to work) are pulling our attention, and our capacity to sustain it, in a million different directions.

For leaders, the stakes are perhaps higher than for most people. Leaders are charged with the stewardship of the organizations and societies in their care. And yet, the attentional demands and information overload that leaders face makes the task of leading increasingly taxing. Between us, we have been working with leaders for the past four decades. Over this time, we have observed that the environment in which leaders operate is becoming ever more complex, fast-paced, uncertain and changeable. A core part of that challenge, as we see it, is the 'always-on' culture that almost every leader needs to operate within. By 'always on', we mean the constant reactivity, hyper-communication and unrelenting pace at which decisions and actions happen. This has been vastly amplified by technology.

The drive to be always on, digesting huge amounts of information and responding to the constant stream of issues, has created, for so many leaders, a distracted, surface-level way of interacting with the world and those they lead. We call this 'info-whelm'. It's a sense in which being fully present is not just difficult; it's almost beyond reach. It's a state where we are both fatigued and scattered at the same time; where our mind feels both exhausted and hyperactive, simultaneously. In this state, we resort to black-and-white thinking, greater reactivity and our decision-making suffers. It is as if we are collectively being swept along in a fast-flowing river trying to keep our heads above water, not knowing how to swim into some still water to catch our breath.

While tech-enabled connectivity has yielded huge benefits in terms of efficiency and flexibility, our view is that these ways of working come at a cost, in terms of leaders' mental health, and the resilience and motivation of those they lead. Technology-mediated ways of working have the potential to unlock great efficiency if used well. But if used poorly, they have profoundly negative impacts on leaders' capacity to think clearly and engage in the strategic and deeply human work of leadership. It is as if technology has been transformed from a reliable servant to a tyrannical master.

In one recent example, we were working with a senior leadership team responsible for the delivery of a large, multimillion-dollar healthcare project. The pressure was huge and the timeframes very intense. The team had been working together for eighteen months in the start-up phase. But people were already feeling very tired and frustrated. This came to a head when an executive on the project, Mike, asked several of his senior managers to attend a snap meeting to iron out some implementation issues that he had concerns about. The team pushed back but Mike dug in, and demanded they be there.[1] He then offloaded on the team and railed about the need for commitment. There was stunned silence in the team.

After a few minutes, Masha, one of the team members spoke up. She tried to point to the deeper issue of fatigue, the need to reconsider how the team works together, and who comes to meetings. In that moment of tension, Mike had his chance to press 'pause' and open up a conversation into the real issue or to just keep pushing. But he had a tonne more things to get through for the rest of the day, with emails and reminders pinging away on his phone. So, he decided not to invest in unpacking his team's concerns. He bulldozed on. In that moment, Mike lacked the awareness to be able to see what was at stake, change gears and address the real issue for his team. He was stuck in overdrive and the moment was missed. The window of opportunity opened and closed, not to open again. As a result, his team and the project rolled on with him, frustrated, tired and increasingly resentful. And sure enough, over the next few months, the resignations started rolling in.

Another assignment involved working with a leader of administrative services in a court. Sadly, the court faced a series of funding cuts, leading to a major restructure and job losses to go with it. For the staff who were left, the workload didn't just remain — if anything it increased, as the list of urgent matters only grew with funding cuts elsewhere in the system. Staff were feeling fatigued, but were also in a state of hyperactivity, almost as if they were running on adrenaline and sheer momentum. It was an unhealthy place to be. A culture had formed that prioritized reactivity and chronic busy-ness, and it was starting to take its toll. Absenteeism increased and several members of the team were on extended sick leave. The manager, Denise, faced a tipping point: either carry on as if there was no alternative, or stop and reset.

Incredibly, Denise was able to see the role she was playing in driving this hyperactive and reactive culture. She could see the train wreck that was coming and thought to rediscover the brake pedal instead of just feverishly pushing the accelerator.

She pulled back from the urgent priorities and brought the team together. Through a series of meetings, the team made some tough decisions and re-prioritized what they did and how they worked. As a part of this, Denise took the time to hear from everyone in the team about what they were personally feeling and seeing.

With a redefined set of priorities for the team, Denise then went to her manager and other key stakeholders in the court to make a case for her team's redefined work plan. This was a game changer. Suddenly, Denise and her team felt like they were in this together and were working with and for each other. Although it was a stressful and taxing period, by taking responsibility for her role in the status quo and having the courage to co-develop a new way of working, she averted disaster for the court and the thousands of people depending on its services. Fundamentally, Denise showed the power of pulling back from one way of working and embracing another that was a more conscious response to the situation.

These stories and their impacts don't just echo what common sense or experience teach us; they exemplify what the science is telling us. In the last few years, there has been an explosion of research into the impacts of mental overload and chronic reactivity on mental health, relationship quality and human performance. In terms of impacts on leaders, this research is only in its infancy. But the trends are emerging.

For example, one study looked at leaders of virtual teams (i.e. managers who only have tech-mediated interactions with their team members) and found that although managers reported delegating more, employees felt the *opposite*. That is, employees felt less control over their work, and also less autonomy (i.e. that their manager was micro-managing them more).[2] More studies are needed to better understand what is driving this 'wedge' in how tech-mediated team members feel at work. But one likely possibility is that managers of virtual teams often feel more cognitively stretched, and less personally connected with those they lead. It might just be that the combination of cognitive overload and social distance can push managers to try to micromanage more — which of course exacerbates the problem. Consistent with this, neuroscience research has found that the overuse of tech-mediated ways of connecting and working disrupts people's higher (executive) functions, such as attention regulation, memory and emotional intelligence, which are all critical to leading well.[3]

Like a foot that is pressing ever harder on the accelerator, what is it that gets us trapped in a state of chronic overdrive? How do we get stuck with the feeling that the only solution to the stress of overdrive is yet more overdrive, task-completion and frenetic activity? What are the impacts of this way of working on ourselves, those we lead and the world we inhabit? And what does it take to turn this around? What does it take as a leader to direct and sustain our attention to where it needs to be, so we have the bandwidth to do the reflecting, planning and deep thinking that are so critical to leadership success? And as leaders, how can we shape our attitude, energy and mindsets, as well as the external work environment, so that we're able to seize those critical moments like the one Denise caught?

In this book, we take a deep dive into the leadership attributes and skills needed to lead well in a hyper-connected environment. Our aim is to provide practical, accessible, evidence-based guidance for busy, high-performing leaders to navigate the challenges of an always-on culture — without losing your team, or yourself, in the process.

As researchers and scientists, we lay out some of the evidence for the impacts of an always-on work culture on leaders' wellbeing, productivity, capacity to sustain themselves, and the impacts of these on the people they lead. As educators and facilitators, we ask you to reflect on key questions and share some of our own observations, experiences and learnings from the field. Finally, drawing on both the science and experience, we provide a set of simple and actionable *tools* and *practices* for leaders to do their best work.

Who is this book for? Leaders everywhere. By itself, having a position of authority does not equal leadership. For us, leaders are people anywhere, in any field of endeavour, who are seeking to influence others to make a difference for the better. But, of course, we most commonly think of leaders as people in positions of authority, that is, people charged with managing teams and organizations. But many people lead in other ways, such as by example, through inspiring others or being thought leaders. Therefore, this book is for all leaders, whether in formal leadership roles or not. This book is also for HR and learning and development professionals wanting to support their organization in navigating the challenges we have previously articulated. Finally, this book is for anyone grappling with the challenges of our hyper-connected work culture, looking to bring greater clarity to the way they work and live.

In this book, each chapter is structured to highlight specific leadership 'capability areas'. For each of the areas we unpack the key issues, some of the scientific evidence, and offer tools for leaders to apply in practice. As lovers of alliteration, we organize chapters in terms of six 'Ps': problem, purpose, priorities, people, personal and progress. In Chapter 1, 'Problem', we lay out the challenges of leading in a hyper-connected environment, examining the science and the key challenges for leaders. In Chapter 2, 'Purpose', we explore some of the impacts of an always-on way of working on leaders' capacity to remain clear on purpose and offer tools for building purpose within high-performing teams and organizations. In Chapter 3, 'Priorities', we unpack some of the impacts of a hyper-connected way of working on leaders' capacity to set priorities, reflect and make good decisions, then offer tools to tackle these challenges. In Chapter 4, 'People', we explore the impacts of technology on leaders' communication and interpersonal relationships, then offer practical strategies for leaders wanting to enhance their interpersonal impact and connection with those they lead, including in remote-work teams. In Chapter 5, 'Personal', we explore some of the impacts of always-on working on leaders' own mental health and capacity to sustain themselves personally and in their professional roles. We then offer practical tips and strategies to promote leaders' health, wellness and energy. Chapter 6, 'Progress', provides a practical 'road map' for leaders wanting to explore these issues with their leadership team, and also with themselves, as part of self-reflection. Finally, Chapter 7 summarizes the book's key takeaways and highlights issues, challenges and opportunities for the future.

Chapter 1

Problem

In this chapter, we unpack some of the challenges of leadership in an age of info-whelm. As we outlined in the Introduction, the demands on leaders' attention seem to have exponentially grown in recent times, often undermining the quality of decision-making and therefore the range of strategic actions leaders have at their disposal. In this environment, what is it that enables a leader to act with clarity? That is, to see through the 'fog of war', gain diverse perspectives and make astute decisions? In politics, government, business and education, these capacities are in great demand. And yet, they are often elusive. As we see it, a key pathway to this kind of clarity — perhaps the most important one — is the way in which leaders deploy their attention. In crises, these challenges are perhaps most clearly laid bare. Let's consider some examples.

Averting a crisis

There was a wave of panic that gripped the world's financial markets in late 2007. As the global financial crisis began its slow but certain train wreck through much of the world's economy, investors, employees and CEOs looked on with horror as to where it all might end. This was a major financial meltdown with huge implications for the so-called 'real world' economy: the jobs and livelihoods of billions of people and families around the globe. In Australia, which is a highly exposed, trade-dependent economy, its so-called 'big four' banks were in crisis discussions with government and regulators as how best to respond. One of these big four banks, Westpac, was led by the nation's first ever female CEO, Gail Kelly. At the peak of the crisis in late 2008 (after the failure of the US bank Lehman Brothers), Kelly was relatively new to the job of CEO having been in the role less than twelve months. The pressure was immense: her job was to keep the bank financially viable, while somehow minimizing the financial blow to the bank's millions of customers and investors.

Kelly knew that she needed to bring a particular kind of 'leadership energy' to the crisis. She understood that if the bank and the nation was to get through this crisis successfully, she needed to bring a calm, focused resolve to everything she did. She describes her approach as a kind of 'compartmentalized' attention, where she was highly disciplined with her attention and her energy. She gave complete attention to the issue or decision at hand, probed deeply and challenged assumptions, and then consciously let that go and moved on to the next task. Kelly describes the fear, emotion and hyperactivity present in the air as a kind of 'white noise' that needed to be noticed, but calmly let go and not given further energy. By working in this way, Kelly describes being able to make all the decisions that were needed, in a timely but well-considered way.[1] Westpac came through the crisis very well and, with government support, was able to minimize the scale of damage wrought on working households and businesses.

The fog of war

Some years back, one of us (Craig), was waiting at a red light on a trip between two university campuses. The light turned green and Craig's car proceeded to move off but then, out of the corner of his eye, he saw another car trying to cross the intersection at speed. The brakes were slammed on but a crash was unavoidable. Thankfully, there were no injuries but the front ends of the two cars were in a sorry state. Details were exchanged and witnesses stopped to give their details confirming that the other driver went through a red light and Craig went through a green one. The other driver confirmed that it was his fault — he was in a rush to get to a meeting he was late for. The situation was resolved amicably enough on the side of the road. Tow trucks came, the cars were taken away and a taxi was hailed to complete the journey.

A few days later, Craig received a letter from the other driver's insurance company saying that information from the other driver suggested that the accident was Craig's fault and action would be commenced to recover the costs. This was an unpleasant surprise, particularly considering that there seemed to be no contention about what happened and everyone seemed to be reasonable and civil after the accident. It was very tempting for the mind to run off into speculation, anger, rumination, worry and strategizing — a veritable fog of thinking. It seemed better to pause and reserve judgment.

Craig passed on the information to his insurance company and they were about to go into battle. But before they did it seemed to Craig that the simplest and most direct route was to call the other driver and simply ask whether he had really claimed that the accident was Craig's fault. The call was made with a cool head, an open mind and a conciliatory attitude. Rather than arguing or accusing, the other driver was contrite and said that he had told his insurance company no such thing. He said to leave it with him. Five minutes later he called back saying that the matter was resolved and his insurance company would pay all costs. What Craig had been sent was a 'standard' letter that was sent out in nearly all cases. Unpleasant as it was to receive such a letter, it was gratifying to resolve the issue through direct communication and a conciliatory attitude. Regretfully, not all such situations are resolved so amicably.

Going into battle with challenges in life and at work is a common enough experience for many of us, but some people must make decisions that have implications for conflict on a far larger scale. If life is complex most of the time, then situations where countries come into conflict with each other are massively complex. Some examples, literally drawn from the fog of war, will illustrate a few points.

October of 1962 was arguably the height of the Cold War. The Soviets had secretly positioned ballistic nuclear missiles in Cuba, some 150 kilometres (90 miles) from the US mainland. John F. Kennedy was the new US president. The situation called for an urgent response. JFK and his administration had inherited a hawkish cadre of senior officials, intelligence experts and military leaders, many of whom, such as senior members of the CIA, pushed for a powerful military response — an airstrike to take out the threat. Having Soviet nuclear missiles in Cuba was a red line in the sand that these officials could not tolerate.

Instead of reacting impulsively and predictably, JFK chose a different tack. He realized the crisis needed a rapid response. The US was under perhaps the greatest existential threat in its history. But he also realized that, because the stakes were so incredibly high, he needed to use all the time and intellectual capacity he had at his disposal to come to a response that was tactically astute. He needed to get a range of divergent options on the table and interrogate them thoroughly. So, he set up a series of meetings with his top aides and advisors. Crucially, he brought in advisors from agencies that had, in the past, been locked out of these kinds of deliberations, typically led by military generals and intelligence chiefs. The President wanted the group to test assumptions, provide counterviews and challenge each other openly. His request was that the group engage in the process as 'sceptical generalists' — dropping their tightly held identities and narrow agendas to take in a wide range of options before they converged on their chosen option.[2]

The group worked intensively, day and night for two weeks, on a response. At last, they narrowed down the many options they considered to two plausible courses of action: a targeted airstrike to take out the Soviet missiles; or a naval blockade of Cuba, to prevent the delivery of further weapons. At the end of the process, the President decided on a naval blockade. The response worked. Envoys were sent in good faith. Each side was suspicious of the other but nobody really wanted a war and a level of trust was established through clear but direct communication. The Soviets subsequently came to the negotiating table and agreed to remove the nuclear missiles from Cuba and the US also secretly agreed to remove its ballistic missiles from Italy, perhaps as a gesture of good faith. De-escalation was achieved. What was it that enabled the US president to take this kind of approach and not go with the impulsiveness and black-and-white mindset he was being pushed into? With the help of a few cool-headed advisors, he was able to pull back from the emotion and visceral sense of threat and see clearly what needed to be done. In that moment, he had clarity.

Soon after the Cuban situation was resolved the US was being drawn into an armed conflict in Vietnam. The Vietnam War was a drawn out and bloody affair. Robert McNamara was the US Secretary of Defence from 1961–68 under Presidents Kennedy and Johnson. As time went on and seeing how disastrously the war was proceeding, McNamara commissioned what became known as the Pentagon Papers. This was an in-depth exploration of the complex and long-running causes of the Vietnam War. These were largely ignored in terms of adapting strategy or ending the war — the war mentality and war machine had too much momentum. The 'sunk-cost bias' was in full swing — the US and its allies were too far in to withdraw no matter how logical a step that appeared to be. Later, in 1995, McNamara visited Hanoi and met his North Vietnamese opposite number during the war, General Võ Nguyên Giáp. They spoke openly and frankly for the first time. Such a conversation 30 years previously could have changed geopolitical history — unfortunately it didn't happen. There was too much mutual distrust. The celebrated 2003 documentary, *The Fog of War: Eleven Lessons from the Life of Robert S. McNamara*, highlighted many of the mistakes and intelligence failures that led to and perpetuated the war. Not least among them was a hawkish attitude and the distrust of the opposition born out of a lack of direct communication.

It would be easy to think that more information alone will lead to better decisions but this is not necessarily so. These days we live in an information age but information is interpreted and misinterpreted based on the psychological disposition of the people using it. A clear, unbiased mind is required to use information well. Following the terrible 9/11 terrorist attacks on the US in 2001 there was an appetite to not only avenge the crimes committed by the terrorists but to finish some unfinished business with Iraq and Saddam Hussein from a decade before. By the early 2000s surveillance technology had come a long way and much of this was being used by President George W. Bush and his advisors to justify what later became the protracted and unsuccessful Iraq War. It was understandable that many in the US and allied countries were experiencing a combination of outrage and fear over what had happened. The main justification for the invasion of Iraq was Iraq's purported possession of weapons of mass destruction. Despite much intelligence being provided to support this contention, it later proved not to be the case. Many cooler heads and world leaders, including a circumspect Robert McNamara, advised against the invasion. Their advice was not listened to and the war proceeded, led by the US in concert with a number of allied countries. In this case it was not a lack of intelligence and information that led to the war but rather an attitude and intense distrust of the opposition that distorted the intelligence in such a way that it was used to reach a conclusion that had likely already been decided. Evidence to the contrary was ignored. This is an example of 'confirmation' and 'anchoring' bias. Like the Vietnam War, the repercussions of these misadventures play out at home and abroad for decades afterwards.

Now we live in the so-called 'information age' where leaders are not just navigating a sea of information but, increasingly, misinformation. Much of this is now coming through social media which is being increasingly weaponized as a pervasive form of propaganda. Whether it is used to justify and defend unjust wars such as the Russian invasion of Ukraine, or cast doubt upon election results in democratic countries, it is being used to inflame emotions, agitate the mind, distort perceptions and confuse the opposition. These forces are drastically complicating the environment leaders operate in.

Like Shakespeare's Hamlet who had his crown usurped by his evil uncle, the mind can become misled, confused and misconstrued. Hamlet describes his state of mind: 'and thus the native hue of resolution is sicklied o'er with the pale cast of thought'. The overloaded mind — whether that load is generated by external or internal forces in the form of overthinking things — makes it harder for us to think clearly enough to know what to do. Information, and the misuse of it, is morphing from the faithful servant to the tyrannical master. If we think making better decisions is merely a matter of having more and more information, then we are likely to be both disappointed and overwhelmed.

Seeing through the fog of war

What is it that enables leaders to pause and respond, rather than react and panic, or be derailed by untested assumptions and false information? The big moments described in the examples above mirror the many thousands of smaller decisions, dilemmas and conflicts that leaders need to navigate week-in, week-out in fulfilling their responsibilities. What are the qualities of attention and attitude that enable a leader to respond with clarity? As we explore in this book, leadership requires — even demands — a certain kind of attention. One that is focused and yet aware and open to divergent perspectives, options, assumptions and opinions. One that is situationally aware and able to 'read the room' — to know when to slow down and when to speed up. Fundamentally, the work of leading calls for conscious responses, and for this, leaders need conscious attention.

From our experience working with leaders in business, government and higher education, conscious attention is in short supply. We learn technical skills at university and build on those as our career unfolds. Leadership models and frameworks are everywhere. But none of this helps you if you are not present — awake and alive to the needs of the moment. What we see is a deficit in this capacity to give, and sustain, conscious attention. This is having a huge impact on leaders' capacity to be their best and do their best work.

But it's not just the attentional *capacities* of leaders that need nurturing (although we unpack these later). As we explore in this book, it is fundamentally an issue with the way work is being done in the information age, and the cultural expectations and norms that come with that. Unparalleled access to, and expectations to continually access, information — enabled by the vast array of tools for collaboration — is changing how work gets done, with big implications for leadership. It is as if modern leaders are in a crisis-like state much of the time.

When leaders become too stretched, they become chronically reactive, revert to black-and-white decision-making, and lack planning and prioritizing.[3] Such an environment degrades a leader's attention. In a state of cognitive overload, a leader also makes unrealistic assumptions and down-plays alternatives. Perhaps most significant of all, when leaders are stretched, they cut corners. This, of course, sets the scene for the ethical scandals we hear about in the news on a regular basis.

The always-on leader

Shiny new tools for collaboration and communication promise to deliver huge amounts of motivation, energy and efficiency. They enable a leader to stay across large volumes of information. They facilitate setting priorities, allocating tasks and monitoring progress. These tools also enable businesses and teams to respond rapidly to changes in the business environment. With this way of working, there's a sense of energy, speed and even mastery as goals are achieved and solutions are developed. But these ways of working also tend to create a kind of energy that preferences doing, reacting and achieving — and not leading. Soon keeping on top of the flood of incoming communications becomes 'the work' and the real work of leadership gets drowned in the deluge.

This is especially the case for people new to a leadership role. Most people with a job have some kind of training that got them there. That is, specific skills that enable them to perform in their job. Over time, with experience, we deepen and grow these skills, perhaps to a point of becoming an 'expert'. For many professionals, we might have deep skills in a few areas, and be able to flexibly learn and grow our skill set into new areas of knowledge. If we are passionate about learning, growth and new challenges, we might be constantly increasing and developing our suite of technical skills. But none of this is leadership.

Once promoted to a leadership role, we're in an entirely new game. It's very easy to feel out of our depth and out of control — especially for the technical expert. A common response is to instinctively bring every ounce of our technical capability to help our team/s solve their problems and, in order that nothing should go wrong, to feel that we both can and should maintain control over all aspects of the job at hand. Feeling overwhelmed and out of our depth, we try to 'out-work' the new role and everyone around us. We essentially put the foot on the accelerator to stay ahead. We ramp up our own (and by extension, our team's) workload and busy-ness, and oftentimes micromanage the work to compensate for our feelings of insecurity and overwhelm.

Even for people who are experienced leaders, there is a common sense of being stretched across too many priorities, accountabilities and information sources. For established managers who might otherwise prioritize face-to-face interactions and more structured ways of working, tech-mediated collaboration and management can feel like an added cognitive load, and even a threat. The pandemic-driven trend toward greater remote or hybrid work has amplified this. A common feeling is that new collaboration tools prioritize tasks and speed over deep problem solving and human interaction.

For many people in leadership roles, getting out of this fast-flowing stream of hyperactivity and reactiveness is very difficult to do. Our technical skills always pull us back in. As does our innate desire for task achievement, and the always-on approach many people feel compelled to embrace. The problem comes, however, when a curve ball arrives. When a more complex people-issue (e.g. mental health, motivation, team dynamics and interpersonal conflict) or an unexpected shock shows up (e.g. changes in strategy, restructures or new technologies), leaders often lack the skills or 'cognitive reserve' to be able to change gear, and deal with them well. Caught in a cycle of doing and reacting, the important strategic and people-work is done poorly — or not done at all.

What drives us to be always-on?

From our work with leaders, and scanning through the research on these issues, we see two main forces that are having a large impact on an always-on way of leading. One force we call 'environmental drivers' and the other we call 'cultural reinforcers'. Each of these forces mutually supports the other, with changes in the work environment triggering work culture changes, which in turn trigger further environmental changes and adaptations. These two forces, in our view, are core to the challenges of always-on work and leadership, but also key to finding solutions.

Environmental drivers

In recent years, the way work gets done has drastically changed. Traditional, more hierarchical ways of structuring the work environment, with a heavy reliance on face-to-face interactions are now well and truly artefacts of the past. Traditional boundaries between senior managers and their teams (e.g. managers having their own office), between discussing and doing (i.e. meetings as opposed to getting work done), and between work and non-work time, have been consciously dismantled. Although these trends have the potential to unlock flexibility and efficiency, there are big downsides that are often overlooked.

A clear example of this is the open-plan office design. Open-plan layouts are designed to enhance connection and collaboration between team members. Managers sit with their employees, creating a level playing field, where, so the idea goes, ideas rather than positional power prevail. These designs create incidental (and uncontrolled) 'encounters', which is meant to mean information is being shared and connections built. But along with these benefits, there are also well-documented costs of open-plan work environments, including people's capacity to focus on tasks, engage in deep thinking and avoid distraction. How often do we hear colleagues say, 'I just get so much more done at home!'?

Studies have found that staff in workplaces with open offices and collocated co-workers typically experience more work interruptions, which undermine the capacity to work on more complex tasks.[4,5] Interestingly, one study found that open-plan offices actually *undermine* face-to-face communication between colleagues.[6] This study tracked the transitions to open-plan offices in two US *Fortune 500* companies and found that face-to-face communication dropped by a staggering 70 per cent. Employees instead reverted to online communication, as they worried about disturbing colleagues and didn't want their incidental conversations being heard by dozens of people within earshot. The apparent connectedness actually pushed people apart and further into discrete, private, online modes of conversation, undermining the very culture that the open-plan was designed to strengthen.

Perhaps a bigger trend, with further reaching impacts, is the explosion of ever more sophisticated online collaboration tools. These tools create virtual workspaces, enabling highly complex collaboration and task management. Tools such as Slack, Asana and Monday.com, to name a tiny sliver of the many offerings in the marketplace, are designed to help plan, deliver and track team members' performance in collaborative work projects. Although these tools can enable big gains in productivity and efficiency, they bring with them several risks and challenges that are not well understood.

With the frequency of notifications and interruptions, the key issue is the impact on people's attention regulation and, as a result, capacity to sustain focus on complex tasks — all core business for any leader. Collaboration tools enable real-time communication, meaning that whenever you are online, you are contactable by your collaborators wherever you are and at any time. You are highly interruptible. According to one recent review of these tools:

> On average, employees at large companies are each sending more than 200 Slack messages per week … Keeping up with these conversations can seem like a full-time job. After a while, the software goes from helping you work to making it impossible to get work done.[7]

Deluged by such messages, the priority shifts from trying to get the work done that we thought we were there to do, to just keeping on top of the flood of so-called 'work' appearing in a variety of inboxes. To get a handle on how many tech-mediated interruptions workers typically face, one group of Australian and UK researchers investigated managers and employees at a large Australian telecommunications company. The researchers found that staff reported, on average, a total of 86 workplace interruptions per day.[8] That's more than ten interruptions per hour in an eight-hour day! These interruptions have a cognitive impact, as the person then needs to recover their focus on what they were doing prior to being interrupted. It's like constantly having to reboot files that have been put on hold. But these interruptions also have a financial impact. For example, a study of knowledge workers in the US (i.e. people working in sectors such as finance, healthcare, education and engineering) found that these workers experienced on average 2.1 hours of daily work interruptions. These disruptions were estimated to cost the US economy $588 billion annually.

In jobs where communication is a key part of the role, these impacts may be even more acute. For example, in the same study of the Australian telecommunications company staff there reported spending on average 5.5 hours per day in communication (e.g. in meetings and technology-mediated communication). This left only two hours per day, on average, for completing tasks. That's a lot of potential hours in the day for interrupting other people and being interrupted!

Lastly, the financial incentives employees face (e.g. financial bonuses and other rewards for performance) can also amplify these impacts. A fascinating study of software engineers who worked at a Fortune 500 company, found that high work interdependence, combined with a competitive financial reward system, caused employees to interrupt each other more frequently.[9] Working with strong financial incentives hanging over your head seems to mean that you become less thoughtful and tactful about how and when you call on colleagues' time and attention.

Related to this, another study of engineers in the US and India found that engineers who said they work in an individualistic work culture, characterized by individual performance incentives, were more likely to view requests from colleagues for help as work *interruptions*, rather than as being a part and parcel of doing their job.[10] In other words, an individualistic work culture seems to heighten the negative impact of work disruptions on people's work. Together, these structural changes in how and where work gets done have created workplace environments where it is very difficult to sustain focus and think deeply.

Cultural reinforcers

In addition to these environmental drivers of the always-on approach, there are cultural reinforcers. These are social expectations, assumptions and patterns of behaviour that exist within workplaces and reinforce the environmental drivers we outlined above. These reinforcers are less tangible and perhaps less obvious than the environmental drivers. But they have a huge impact on how any individual engages in their work.

As one example, the transition from desktop to mobile technology for getting work done (an 'environmental driver') has seen big shifts in expectations from managers about when and where staff respond to messages, and the volumes of work that are being done after hours. These expectations are often unspoken and form a self-reinforcing culture where people collaborate after hours, creating a collective sense of this being the norm — and even the expectation. Once the majority of people in a team or business work this way, it gets harder and harder for people who do not or cannot work after hours to set boundaries. There's a form of social expectation for working late even if the company or team has explicitly said, 'people can choose when they work'. Because we are social creatures, these social 'undercurrents' can be very hard to resist although they are often not articulated.

One study interviewed 48 knowledge professionals in the UK about the flexibility that technology brings.[11] Strikingly, these researchers uncovered what they called a 'paradox of autonomy': while constant work-connectivity made people *think* they have greater autonomy and flexibility to work at times and in places that suit them, in practice it had the opposite effect. These professionals felt increasingly bound and controlled as they experienced a growing social pressure to respond quickly, and at any time, to work issues because this had become the norm across the business. The initial appeal of this apparent freedom quickly turned into the tyranny of expectation to respond everywhere and always.

Another issue is organizational 'polychronicity', or the extent to which employees feel their organization values and prioritizes multitasking.[12] This practice is even written into many job descriptions as a 'desirable attribute'. The online world has arguably made multitasking more ubiquitous and complex than ever before. Rather than trying to (just) write and listen in a meeting, online collaboration means people have many,

many tasks, across multiple platforms, all in play at the same time, switching (or often reacting) between them, as messages and prompts come in. As a result, multitasking has arguably become far more complex and cognitively demanding than ever before. This way of working has become the norm, and even the expectation, in many organizations. It has the allure of making it appear we will get more done and also have a fuller life.

These cultural reinforcers may be even greater in roles and workplaces that are highly competitive and performance oriented. They are also more powerful in countries or sectors that lack strong institutions protecting balanced workloads (e.g. unions, job security, etc.) and where there is a huge demand for well-paid jobs and not enough jobs to go around. In these settings, work pressures can be immense, meaning employees feel culturally compelled to stay connected to their work and respond to messages after hours, just to keep their job. This trend has led, in part, to a phenomenon known as 'smartphone dependence', driven by the need to stay connected to work around the clock.

One recent study explored smartphone dependence among Chinese employees. In this study, researchers surveyed 10,233 Chinese white-collar professionals. The study found that as many as 80 per cent of these professionals had developed a high level of smartphone dependency, feeling the need to stay connected with their workplace outside of working hours in order to be seen to be doing their job.[13] In Korea, research has found that 70 per cent of Korean employees regularly use their smartphones outside of their regular work hours to get their work done.[14] Another study of employees in Korea found that employees' work-related smartphone use after work hours was linked to higher rates of burnout, and this burnout was amplified where employees felt their work environment did not support them.[15] Although this is very much a global phenomenon, these cultural reinforcers of an always-on way of working seem to be heightened in industries and countries where the pressures on individuals are much higher.

Together, these cultural assumptions, expectations, and pressures around responsiveness, multitasking and media-use appear to strongly reinforce the environmental drivers of an always-on way of working. Next, let's explore some of the downstream human impacts of such a work culture.

Downstream human impacts

In terms of the human impacts of an always-on way of working, the scientific research points to a kind of 'chronic disruption' of people's sense of mental clarity, capacity to respond to complexity, quality of decision-making, and sense of connection and enjoyment at work. We see three main ways in which these potential downsides are felt among professionals:

» Cognitive impacts.
» Wellbeing impacts.
» Social impacts.

Cognitive impacts

Perhaps the most widely explored impact of an always-on way of working is the effect on cognition. In almost every job, there is a need to be able to focus attention on the task at hand, prioritize, make decisions and plan. For leaders, these skills are fundamental to what it means to lead others. A growing body of science over the past decade has begun to highlight the ways in which always-on work impacts our cognitive capacities. Here, we point to just a couple of examples.

Cognitive neuroscience research has shone a fascinating light on the problem of leaders' capacity to prioritize. Some of the first research in this area was done by Clifford Nass at Stanford University. Nass and his team wanted to understand the impact of 'media multitasking' on people's ability to engage in more complex cognitive work tasks. For many of us, we spend most of our day working intensely across multiple collaboration platforms and communication channels, as well as working across multiple devices (smartphones, laptops and other media). But does the *way* we engage with this kind of work matter? Is there a difference between those of us who find ourselves switching rapidly and reactively between apps and devices (as we're told, *actual* multitasking, or doing two things at once, is a myth), and those of us who are able to stay on-task and are less distractible? In 2009, Nass and his team ran a landmark study on this question. They showed that people who are chronic 'media multitaskers' (i.e. regularly try to do multiple tasks simultaneously via media/

devices) performed substantially *worse* on complex cognitive tasks and tests of working memory than those who do not multitask. Rather than getting better at multitasking, Nass found that chronic multitaskers' cognitive performance actually got *worse* the more they did it.[16]

Studies since then have replicated this basic finding: trying to stretch our attention across too much information simultaneously undermines our cognitive performance (e.g. poor memory, impaired decision making, higher stress, increased errors, poorer communication). For example, a recent study of US knowledge workers found that when employees used email or other text communication to solve complex problems, this undermined their performance not just on the task at hand, but also on subsequent complex or ambiguous work tasks.[17] It appears that using tech-enabled communication to engage with complex problems generates a 'cognitive deficit' that spills over and hurts our capacity to use our important executive functions for other tasks. Research on the effect of multitasking on reading comprehension and reading time shows a negative effect on both, especially when time is limited.[18] We might think we're going to get more done, but the opposite is true.

Wellbeing impacts

Another impact of always-on work is on how we feel at work and beyond. The inability to switch off and disconnect leaves us feeling a chronic sense of pressure and guilt, even when we're wanting to switch off. This feeling is often not linked to any particular issue, but an underlying feeling of needing to be doing or responding — and has been labelled the 'attention deficit trait'. This can also, of course, be tied to a specific issue or problem, and we find ourselves mulling over it at all times of the day — and night! Studies on this have begun to identify a few different impacts. One is more immediate: when we're trying to do too many things at once (i.e. multitask), we feel a sense of emotional imbalance and frustration. For example, a study of multitasking in the US found that regular media multitaskers displayed more impulsiveness and less executive control and ability to regulate their emotions.[19] Another study in the US looked at not just multitasking, but at people who are heavily invested in mobile devices more broadly, and again found that people who are more invested in their mobile devices showed more impulsive behaviour and less capacity to delay gratification.[20]

Another effect, which is more cumulative, is 'device dependence', discussed above. This is a more general sense of needing to be connected and checking work constantly. The research on this shows us that when we feel this kind of dependence on our devices, we have worse mental health (i.e. experience more stress, ruminate more and feel more anxiety).[21] Also, device dependence has been linked to having lower self-esteem, and even less hope.[22] Lastly, longitudinal studies have found that online dependency is linked to worse emotion regulation. For example, research that we have conducted has found that the compulsive use of devices consistently leads to difficulties in regulating emotions, including less emotional intelligence, and difficulties pursuing goals in the presence of negative emotions.[23] These are critical skills for leaders, who need to be able to regulate their emotional reactions to situations to maintain team focus and cohesion.

Social impacts

A third impact of always-on work is its effect on our social connections. Humans are fundamentally social creatures, and technology has massively increased our capacity to communicate with each other. This connectivity can build our sense of being in a community and sharing experiences with other people. But at the same time, large volumes of very superficial, task-based communication may not add much to that sense of connection — it may even erode it. Research has begun trying to understand how intensive media use impacts this sense of connection and social support. For work teams and their leaders, this is critically important in building a connected, collaborative work environment.

As an example, a study in the US looked at how people's smartphone use impacted their sense of connectedness and social support. The researchers found that smartphone use for direct, person-to-person interactions increased people's sense of connectedness, as you might expect. But interestingly, when people became addicted to their device (known as 'problematic smartphone use'), this effect flipped over, and they felt *less* tangible support from people in their social network. This is likely because people's online activity and more superficial communication displaced their authentic connection with their core sources of social support (family, friends and colleagues, etc.). So, rather than increasing connection, we become less connected and supported if we become overly dependent on our devices.

What does this mean for leaders?

The research on these issues is rapidly unfolding, uncovering new and important insights in how we interact with technology, and the impacts of this on our capacity to lead. In this chapter, we have highlighted a few areas where we see these impacts showing up most clearly — cognitive capacities, wellbeing and social connection. However, rather than just highlighting the problem, our intention is to explore how leaders and their organizations can manage these challenges: taking the best of what technology brings, without sacrificing ourselves or those we care about in the process. In the rest of this book, we unpack in more depth what we see as being the core tasks of leadership — purpose, priorities, people and personal — and lay out the critical leadership skills organizations need to cultivate to remain successful in the 21st century. We dedicate separate chapters to each of these 'Ps' of leadership.

At the end of each subsequent chapter, we include a section outlining a range of easy-to-implement personal skills and several policy recommendations arising from what has been covered that are aimed at addressing the issues explored. In this way, if you choose, you can work through this book like a workbook, perhaps by reading one chapter per week or fortnight, and establishing the skills before moving onto the next chapter. Our goal is to provide a set of practical tools, habits and skills that leaders can cultivate so that you, your team and your organization can thrive.

Chapter 2

Purpose

As many people will recall, July 2018 saw the remarkable rescue of twelve boys and their soccer coach from a vast cave network in remote Thailand. The boys had been at soccer practice and decided to explore the cave. They had been in the cave many times before. However, this time, they got themselves into some trouble. Unbeknown to them it started to rain outside, and the cave began to fill with water. It was the peak of the wet season. The boys' pushbikes were found abandoned outside the cave. Locals sounded the alarm. The news of the lost boys and their coach quickly captured international media attention, as the Thai authorities grappled with trying to locate the group inside a massive cave network in a remote mountainous area that was rapidly filling with water.

As the news spread, governments from around the globe began offering assistance. Technical experts, engineers, logistics experts and geologists were enlisted to help devise a strategy for finding the group and, if alive, somehow getting them out. The Thai government set up a command centre outside the cave and began coordinating the various elements of the Thai military, police and emergency rescue services, and volunteers, as well as the international experts who were flown in.

Leading the effort was the governor of the Chang Rai province, a man by the name of Narongsak Osatanakorn. With so much media attention, so many offers of help, and a huge swathe of around 10,000 volunteers, Osatanakorn's leadership of the rescue was critical. He knew that they were racing against the clock. But, to have the best chance of success, everyone needed to be aligned and totally committed to the job. Early on in the operation, Osatanakorn was reported to have said to the group of rescue workers and volunteers:

> *Anyone who cannot make enough sacrifices can go home and stay with their families. You can sign out and leave straight away. I will not report any of you. But for those who want to work, you must be ready any second. Just think of them as our own children.[1]*

What did this statement do? It focused the rescuer's attention on a) whether they wanted to be there, and b) why they were there. Through his communication, Osatanakorn clarified the purpose of what they were there to do, stripped it down to its essence. The statement also delivered a powerful 'emotional ground' from which all decisions and actions could be taken, for anyone working on the rescue. 'Just think of them as your own children.'

There was unity of purpose and unity of command. The team, led by the Thai authorities and aided by international experts, set about working out how they could find the boys. In the end, they decided to send cave divers in to look for them. On the ninth day, to the world's disbelief, the boys and their coach were found alive. They had survived mainly because of two things. First, by drinking from tiny trickles of fresh water running down the side of the cavern they were stranded in. Second, the coach was an experienced meditator and taught the boys to stay present, be inwardly calm and conserve energy throughout the ordeal. As a result, the boys were in remarkably good shape physically and mentally when they were found.

From there, a high-risk plan was devised to sedate each of the boys (who couldn't swim), and after fitting them in wetsuits and oxygen masks, guide them through the dark, coffee-coloured waters of the cave system. Tragically, the day before the rescue operation was to commence, a Thai Navy SEAL died, while he was depositing oxygen masks along the treacherous route. This highlighted to all just how dangerous and uncertain the rescue operation was going to be.

But Osatanakorn decided to push ahead with the rescue plan. The boys' health would start to deteriorate if they delayed for the weeks and weeks it would take for the waters to recede — and even this was not guaranteed. Led by Australian cave divers and medics, Dr Craig Challen and Dr Richard Harris, the team started the recovery operation. Somehow, the system worked. One by one, the boys and the coach were sedated and brought out. After an eight-day operation to extract them, all twelve boys and their coach were out safely.

What was it about Osatanakorn's leadership that delivered success? There were obviously many factors at play, including a very large element of good fortune. But within the operation itself, smooth execution was by no means guaranteed. Between the different Thai organizations involved (e.g. the Navy SEALs, police, local medical teams and regional government officials), as well as the 10,000 volunteers and international experts, the whole effort could have become mired in conflict, poor decision-making, and the death of the boys. Yet, the Thai rescue head was able to focus the attention of these disparate actors on their core mission — their purpose — and calmly keep people engaged with that.

A compelling need

In times of crisis, this kind of laser focus is arguably relatively easy to generate. Osatanakorn even referred to the rescue operation as a 'war'. There was a clear and present danger, and the contrast between success or failure was in sharp relief. Put another way, there was a clear and compelling *need* around which everything else could be organized. But how does a leader of any operation, team or project keep this kind of laser focus, when the compelling need is much less clear, or even seems non-existent? How do leaders sustain the performance and commitment of their teams over the long haul, or where the impacts of the work are much less tangible?

Consider Genevieve. She leads a team of around 50 clerks and financial officers at a large global bank, based in Miami, Florida. Her team's job is to ensure that when the bank makes new loans to its corporate customers, the legal and regulatory 'back end' of these deals is done correctly, and the appropriate fiduciary and regulatory checks are in place. Does that sound inspiring? Genevieve's team essentially processes paperwork. They follow up with other parts of the bank to get sign-off or missing information and enter it into a massive database. In fact, their work is vitally important for the smooth functioning of the bank, and the bank is vital for the financial viability of many people's lives, but the team members are not conscious of this.

Genevieve is new in her leadership role and quickly realizes her team are not well connected to any sense of purpose. In fact, over the past three months around one third of the team has left, and she is struggling to fill positions. Genevieve decides to act. With help from colleagues in HR, she designs a set of conversations with her team, to articulate what their core function is within the business, and why their work matters. She seeks people's input and ideas. Rather than focusing on the bank, Genevieve focuses her team's attention on the core needs or problems that *they, as a team,* exist to solve.

After weeks of refinement, they land on a simple statement that reads:

> *We exist to support the financial health and prosperity of families, communities, schools and businesses, right around the United States and the world. We provide an amazing experience to everyone we serve. We take pride in our work, are well rewarded for what we do, and are committed to supporting each other, to do our best work.*

The members of Genevieve's team were able to expand their view from a narrow focus into a vision. At the same time, she helped them pinpoint their core reason for being — the fundamental needs they exist to serve. It isn't rescuing children from a cave, but it was, for Genevieve and her team, something they could get out of bed for each day and know why they were going to work: the financial health and prosperity of the families, schools, communities and businesses they serve.

As well as this, Genevieve and her team articulated some more tangible or proximate motivations. They committed to providing amazing service for their key stakeholders, taking pride in their work and being well rewarded for it, and also supporting each other. These more tangible, immediate purposes are important, especially when they connect with the ultimate, 'big picture' aims. Also, there was an integrity to these tangible statements. By including 'we are well rewarded for what we do', they acknowledged that for many in the team, a core part of their purpose is providing for their families and building their own financial security. They acknowledged this motivation and made it explicit.

As Genevieve's case illustrates, to generate a clear purpose, leaders still need to connect their people and resources to a compelling need. It's just that how you do that, and how you keep it compelling, is going to be different from when you're in a crisis. From our experience working with teams in the armed forces, emergency services and in business, leaders need to be constantly adjusting and refreshing how they connect with their organization's purpose as conditions change and as people in the organization come and go. A bit like a dancer, who intimately follows the movement of their partner, the leader wants to be awake and alert to the changing needs and conditions of their team or organization and respond to that. Although purpose is generally a relatively stable 'compass point', the route to getting there needs to be kept fresh. A purpose must be living. To keep it alive and fresh, it needs to be tied to a need and serve something bigger than the individuals involved.

Intrinsic motivation

Decades of research on human motivation has lots to teach us about purpose. This research has provided some very rich insights into the kinds of 'psychological ingredients' leaders need to have in their purpose 'mix', to ensure it is engaging and relevant, and can cut through the noise in an information-saturated environment. At the heart of this is the distinction between intrinsic and extrinsic motivation. Intrinsic motivation refers to doing something because of the inherent satisfaction it brings or because it aligns with deeply held personal values. Extrinsic motivation refers to doing something primarily because of an external reward.

When people experience intrinsic motivation, they experience engagement, vitality, joy and satisfaction in what they do. They are more committed and dedicated. By contrast, when people are extrinsically motivated, they are driven more by external incentives, such as approval, social status, image, power and influence, wealth, or avoiding the loss of these things. A large body of scientific research shows that when people are primarily driven by extrinsic motivators, they tend to be less happy, satisfied, and are less likely to persist in the face of difficulty.[2] Extrinsic motivators, such as pay rises, social status and promotions focus our attention on getting the reward we want, meaning that once we have the reward, our motivation and effort tends to fall away and we are not sustained energetically or emotionally in the face of adversity. Intrinsic motivators, on the other hand, have the opposite effect — they sustain us even when rewards are not immediately forthcoming or when we are facing adversity.

The job of the leader, then, is to provide a sense of purpose that is *intrinsically motivating*. When people feel connected to a sense of why they do what they do, and why it matters, they are more intrinsically motivated. The motivation is 'internalized'– that is, integrated into the person's sense of self, identity, and what they value. A core task of the leader is to help people to connect with or 'internalize' a shared sense of mission, purpose and values.

The neuroscience is also fascinating here. When people experience more intrinsic forms of motivation, this triggers the activation of dopamine neurons in the brain, which is one of the brain's 'reward system' responses.[3] It's a 'feel good' neurotransmitter. Dopamine release is linked with a host of good things, like positive emotions, cognitive flexibility, creativity and greater persistence on tasks.[4,5] Also, neuroimaging studies have found that intrinsic motivation activates a region in the brain that is called the 'executive network'.[6] The executive network is like the leadership level of the brain and it is critical for our ability to focus and control our attention, to think strategically and to regulate our responses and impulses — all critical in any leadership role. These neuroimaging studies have also found that when we are intrinsically motivated, we experience *less* activity in the 'default network' of the brain.[7] The default network tends to be activated when we are distracted and operating on automatic pilot. It is responsible for ruminating and mind-wandering, and long-term over-activation has been linked to the onset of dementia.[8]

Together, this neuroscience research suggests that when leaders facilitate a compelling sense of purpose and mission that intrinsically motivates people, their staff will be far more dedicated, focused, disciplined and also more likely to persist in their work. These benefits are even more stark in a work environment that is frantic and always-on, and where autopilot can easily be the default way of working. In these work settings, the attributes of intrinsic motivation are more critical than ever.

Authentic engagement

One other aspect of building a clear and motivating sense of purpose is authenticity — the quality of being genuine, real or true to oneself and to others. When people see this quality in a leader they tend to respect and trust it. By being authentic and honest, leaders can cut through the noise and distraction and create a unified purpose. By going straight to the emotional 'core' of what they were doing, the Thai rescue commander was able to engage the rescue team around a unified purpose. In the example of Genevieve's team, the core purpose of the work was emphasized first with 'We exist to support the financial health and prosperity of families, communities, schools and businesses, right around the United States, and the world.' But acknowledging that the team commits to 'being well rewarded for what we do' was also really important for people in the team. Although this was perhaps a more extrinsic driver, it was authentic. And it tied back to a deeper need for people in the team: providing for their family and having the resources to be able to enjoy life. By getting to that underlying need, even an extrinsic driver becomes more intrinsically rewarding and motivating.

The key difference lies in *how* these motivational drivers — both intrinsic and extrinsic — are arrived at. Where these are imposed from the top down, and people do not feel a sense of owning or valuing them and there is no bigger picture, you don't get great buy-in — even for so-called 'noble' and 'for purpose' mission statements. These things cannot be imposed from the top down. They need to be explored and co-developed. Similarly for extrinsic motivators. Not understanding 'why' an extrinsic carrot (or stick) is offered, people chase the reward, or rush to meet the target, without ever knowing why it matters. However, when, like with Genevieve's team, intrinsic and extrinsic drivers are identified and are 'owned' by the team itself, and are linked to an underlying need, they can be powerful motivators.

To summarize, a clear and shared sense of purpose builds intrinsic motivation. This has huge benefits in terms of staff engagement and performance. At the same time, a sense of purpose needs to be authentic and connected to tangible needs. The astute leader works out how to connect their team to the intrinsic motivation first (e.g. serving customers, or taking pride in the quality of our work) and also ensures that extrinsic motivators (e.g. financial reward) work towards and not against that primary purpose.

Based on the research and our experience, leaders need to help people connect with the underlying needs that these various motivators are based on.

The challenge of leading with purpose

Having laid out the context, we now unpack three broad challenges that we believe are critical to embedding purpose within a team or organization *and* are made more difficult in an always-on, information-saturated work environment. The first challenge is how a leader *consciously clarifies* a clear sense of purpose within their team or organization. The second is the way a leader keeps this sense of purpose and intent *fresh, clear and tangible.* And the third challenge is how leaders and their teams use purpose to *solve complex problems.*

While these challenges are not new by any means, they can be tough to overcome in fast-paced work environments where people are geographically dispersed and highly results-oriented. Added to this is the very common scenario in many workplaces where the work we do today is not clearly linked to a tangible or 'human' outcome tomorrow (i.e. where the individuals within the team cannot feel or touch the impact of what they do). In remote work environments, and many sectors of the modern economy, this is the norm. In this kind of context, how can a leader a) cut through the noise and busy-ness and b) connect people to a compelling, living need? These are indeed big challenges. Below, we unpack each of these and provide a set of *focus* questions for leaders to consider in terms of how they approach the issue of purpose.

1. Clarifying purpose

Over the last decade, researchers have begun trying to understand how leaders build and sustain shared purpose in their organizations, and the impact of an always-on culture on this. This research tries to understand the various ways in which intensive technology use affects leaders' capacity to support and get the best out of those they lead. One big issue is what is known as 'technostress'. This is where we feel the technological demands of our work, including online communication, is making our work *harder* rather than easier. It's where we feel overwhelmed and stressed by technology at work.

One recent study at a US company found that when managers experienced technostress (i.e. felt overwhelmed and stressed by technology in their work), they resorted to more 'transactional leadership' behaviours.[9] As the name suggests, transactional leadership is where a leader views their relationship with their team as transactional and task-bound, and focuses their leadership on progressing tasks. There is nothing wrong with this per se, but transactional leadership does not focus on the more human element of leadership, such as promoting the growth and development of staff, meeting personal needs or providing a clear sense of meaning or purpose in the work. The motto of transactional leadership could be described as: 'get in, get the job done, and get out again'.

Even more concerning, another study of US leaders found that leaders experiencing 'technostress' were more likely to default to 'laissez-faire' approaches to leadership. Laissez-faire leadership involves disengaging and neglecting the basic task of setting goals and ensuring teams deliver. This approach definitely neglects clarity of purpose in a team. It is a 'hands-off' and 'stand-off' kind of leadership. This research aligns with the experience of many teams we've worked with: when leaders feel highly overloaded and 'technostressed', leading stops. The overload of information leads to an excessively high cognitive load, which in turn leads to poorer decision-making and lower creativity.[10,11]

Take the example of Michelle. She runs a startup that has gone from a small team of four software engineers to a larger team of 25 to 30 staff. To help make the transition to a larger business and to better coordinate who is doing what tasks, Michelle and her team use two online collaboration apps to manage their work and projects and respond rapidly to new priorities. They have a very flat team structure, where people are empowered to make decisions and take initiative. Michelle's staff are highly engaged, proactive and do great work. However, over time, cracks have started to emerge within the team. The culture developed within the business is to just automatically say 'yes', and to 'make it happen'. But as the company has grown over the past two years, people's workloads have steadily increased. The surface-level culture of up-beat energy, positivity and fun, seems to hide deeper issues of fatigue, exhaustion and even burnout. Michelle is hugely stretched running the growing business. Her challenge, then, is to pull back from the day-to-day 'busywork' and create the space for more honest conversations about what staff are currently feeling, and what needs to shift.

When leaders pull back and actively cultivate a clear sense of purpose and a set of principles for how and when work gets done, people feel less reactive and pressured. A study of leaders in the US specifically looked at the problem of 'workaholism' — that is, staff finding it difficult to disengage mentally from work.[12] It is sometimes confused with being an aspect of 'work engagement'. Workaholism is different to being passionate about your work. Passion and enthusiasm are healthy. Workaholism is when passion and enthusiasm get out of control and morph into obsession and/or addiction to work. When we become so consumed by our work to the extent that we cannot switch off, we end up sacrificing other important parts of our life such as family, exercise and sleep. This study found that when employees have clarity around their work's purpose, the harmful impacts of workaholism are dampened, and team members are better able to switch off from work and speak up when they need to. It's as if a clear sense of purpose helps people to have a clear 'compass' about their work and are guided more by that than the immediate 'sugar hit' we get from hitting highly ambitious short-term targets (at the expense of our long-term health).

One of the main reasons that mindfulness-based interventions are so useful for improving work performance and wellbeing at the same time is that mindfulness helps a person to be present — not only when they are working but also in the rest of their non-working life.[13] This makes space for mental downtime and renewal.

Other studies have shown that being clear about your values and purpose builds a kind of buffer against burnout and disengagement. For example, one meta-analysis (i.e. a crunching together of many similar studies into one big study) looked at workplace programs designed to sharpen employees' purpose and clarity on their values. The researchers found that values-strengthening programs consistently resulted in employees experiencing less stress and burnout symptoms.[14] It seems that clarity of values acts as a kind of 'inoculation' against stress.

This aligns with other studies showing that when people have a clear sense of purpose and meaning (known as 'eudaemonic' wellbeing, from the ancient Greeks), they are less likely to feel stressed and get sick. This research studied the body's immune cells and found that eudaemonic wellbeing reduced the body's expression of inflammatory genes, which have been linked to chronic stress.[15] At the same time, eudaemonic wellbeing *increased* the production of antiviral genes, central to maintaining good immunity. So, it seems that purpose is good for not just our motivation, but also our health!

Given these challenges, how can leaders cultivate a shared and clear sense of purpose within their team or business, especially in an attentionally 'crowded' environment where people's attention is stretched across so many priorities and deliverables? Strategies and approaches are going to vary from business to business. Instead of providing prescriptions, below are a set of *focus questions* you can consider in deciding how you approach the issue of purpose.

Focus Question 1. What is the core need or needs we exist to serve? Purpose needs a clear sense of why the business or organization exists. Thinking back to the Thai cave rescue example, every organization needs to figure out what actual need they exist to serve, and why that matters. This sense of compelling need needs to be clear, tangible and focused. Another way of putting this uses the work of Edgar Schein, Professor at Sloan School of Management at MIT and famous thinker on organizational culture. Schein says leaders need to ask themselves: What are the problems that this team or organization exists to solve?[16] By being clear on these problems, the team or business can organize itself to solve them — including creating a work culture that supports that. The core challenge with this is boiling down the core need or needs that the organizations exist to address. You want this to be sharp and focused, not diffuse or vague. The clearer and more tangibly you can articulate these needs, the more compelling and motivating this will be.

Focus Question 2. How am I engaging my team or organization around purpose? Senior leaders often go away and develop a clean, polished set of statements on purpose that don't speak to or for people across the rest of the organization. So, the process of clarifying and refining that sense of core purpose is as important as the outcome itself. Leaders do well to think carefully about the process they design for, reflecting on purpose, harvesting feedback, turning purpose into actions/behaviours/initiatives within the business, and then revisiting these issues on a regular basis. In a fast-paced environment, people typically need to take some time out and away from their daily work to consider these questions deeply. A sense of purpose needs to be shared, co-owned and key stakeholders need to feel they have a voice. The people who work in the team or organization are like its eyes and ears and if they cannot freely and honestly provide feedback and information then the leader is less able to see and hear what they need to. Often people talk about missing 'the real conversation'. As a leader, you want people to feel safe enough to have the 'real conversation' in the room with you, rather than in the corridors. The leader plays a critical role here in cultivating this sense of safety and trust. Crucially, people need to feel a sense of psychological safety, so that they can be honest about the factors and drivers that motivate them, and why these matter. Psychological safety is like the 'container' or 'room' within which people in the organization engage with each other. It is the conditions under which you operate. You don't want everyone huddling in the middle of the metaphorical room, afraid to speak honestly. Instead, you want people to feel free to walk around the room, exploring the décor, peering out the windows, and conversing openly with each other.

Focus Question 3. How authentic are we being? While a statement of purpose is external as well as internal facing, it needs to be authentic and real for those who create it. Otherwise, it is, at best, window dressing and, at worst, potentially deceptive. For example, many companies have been accused of 'greenwashing' their image, rather than having an authentic commitment to the environment and sustainability.[17] There is often a temptation to articulate a company's purpose essentially as a marketing tool: something that sounds impressive and will appeal to customers. Appealing to customers is, of course, critical. But in doing this, you don't want to sacrifice authenticity; that clarity on why the business exists for those who have a stake in it. For most businesses, winning customers is one of multiple motivations. Other motives might be creating strong and sustainable shareholder value; becoming field-leaders in a particular service or product; generating game-changing innovations that create lasting value; building a reputation as a knowledge leader in the industry; creating an organizational culture that is rewarding and inclusive; or rewarding people generously for their great work. The bottom line is that you want your purpose statement to capture the essence of why the business exists (i.e. the core needs it serves), not just one appealing or marketable aspect, ignoring other important elements. People can easily and quickly tell if a statement of purpose is too formulaic and lacks authenticity, if it is too polished and clinical, or even too altruistic in tone. In the current environment, where questions of purpose have become a key priority for many businesses, we see this problem. The business might have a compelling and inspiring purpose statement, but how does it link to what the firm actually does and why its people work there? To what extent does the purpose statement actually inform the strategic decisions the business takes? This all points back to the integrity of the statement, and how well it embodies what the organization's leaders and staff really feel, believe and do.

2. Keeping it fresh and tangible

The second challenge for leaders in an always-on work environment is keeping your collective purpose fresh and tangible. In a fast-paced business, one of the biggest challenges is how to embed your purpose so it 'shines' through every decision and action staff and leaders undertake. In our experience, this is why people often feel a sense of resentment or frustration around any effort to explore the issue of purpose. They see it as tokenistic and not a good use of their time. And very often, they are right! Done poorly, work on purpose just alienates and frustrates people. This is even more so in high-pressure work environments where people are already very stretched just keeping on top of their core tasks. The challenge for a leader is to think carefully about how purpose is made real, tangible and kept fresh and relevant. Here, we explore a few questions leaders can ask themselves to keep purpose fresh.

Focus Question 4. How and when am I communicating purpose? Perhaps the simplest and most powerful way of embedding and reinforcing purpose within a team or organization is for its leaders to be regularly talking about and encouraging it. If the team leader or CEO is not regularly referring to, acting in alignment with, and reinforcing the organization's shared purpose and values it sends a very clear message to staff that these things are not important; they are 'window dressing'. Conversely, by using purpose and values to inform strategic decisions, by regularly exploring a core value of the company (e.g. highlighting ways in which individuals or teams have been embodying it), discussing why it matters, and by providing recognition for staff who embody these values, leaders put the company's values 'in the water supply'. Leaders need to think carefully about how and when they will communicate and reinforce purpose across the organization. In support of this, a recent study of employees at a market-leading and fast-paced logistics company found that when their leaders engaged in 'transformational leadership' behaviours (i.e. reinforcing a clear sense of shared sense of purpose and an elevating mission), employees experienced less 'technostress' in their work, and felt less fatigued and frustrated by the demands of technology in their work.[18] By regularly connecting with purpose, these transformational leaders were able to cut through some of the impacts of an always-on work culture, and help people to stay clear on why their job matters.

Focus Question 5. Do my behaviours consistently embody our purpose and values? As the regular news feed of corporate scandals shows us, communicating purpose is meaningless if leaders are not living their organization's purpose and values in their actions and decisions. Unless leaders are actually *being* the purpose they espouse, all of the above is meaningless. This is where having a clear set of values and linked behaviours that are widely owned across the organization is invaluable. In this way, the values become embodied in the workplace culture. Clear values and standards of behaviour provide a yardstick against which everyone, including leaders, can be held accountable. If 'purpose' is your collective 'why', values are your collective 'how', and an agreed set of values-aligned behaviours are your 'what'. Values are a set of principles that make clear how you want to function as a team or an organization. They are high-level qualities of behaviour, such as 'acting with courage', 'showing empathy' and 'tolerating failure' that the organization holds as important. The values-aligned behaviours (i.e. the 'what') are a relatively narrow set of behaviours that will bring to life the organization's core values and pull towards its purpose (we discuss these further below, under *Focus Question 6*).

Due to their level of influence, leaders need to be role-modelling these behaviours and values every day. Leaders need to demonstrate them in the way they respond to situations, engage with their staff and customers, and make decisions. For this role-modelling to work, leaders need to think carefully about their visibility. Role-modelling can only happen when leaders *connect* with their employees, so thinking carefully about how visible you are, and when and how these 'connection points' happen, is critical to embedding purpose and values. Initially, this requires effort and constant vigilance until it is hardwired into the leader's brain, but with consistency it is hardwired into the workplace's culture. Then it becomes relatively easy to maintain it. In an online work environment, and especially in a hyper-paced one, opportunities for authentic connection can be constrained or squeezed out amongst the busyness. So, leaders do well to consciously design and schedule the face-to face-touch points, online touchpoints and other communications that will embed purpose. Perhaps the most telling, though, are the 'connection points' that are unscheduled. This is one of the great advantages of face-to-face engagement with work colleagues and one of the main disadvantages of purely virtual work environments.

Focus Question 6. How do we support and hold each other accountable for our purpose and values? Another important area for leaders and their teams to consider is how will we hold each other accountable for acting in line with our purpose and values? One simple way is to articulate a narrow set of behaviours that reflect your organization's values that you can richly reward and also hold each other accountable against (i.e. the 'values-aligned behaviours' we mentioned above). This set of behaviours should ideally be quite focused. The longer the list gets the greater the chance you have of overwhelming people, losing focus and diluting the potency of the message. Be selective. You want to isolate a handful of critical behaviours that will either 'make or break' your core values. These behaviours serve as markers or signposts for your core values and help people to know how they are tracking in either upholding or undermining the organization's core purpose and values. Examples of values-aligned behaviours that we have seen teams identify include: 'We listen attentively'; 'We take a generous view of situations'; 'We support people speaking the unvarnished truth in a respectful way' and 'We always focus on delivering results but flag implementation problems early'. Having a small set of explicit behaviours also provides excellent accountability for the leader: the team can also assess the leader against this set of core behaviours. The team can build check-ins on these behaviours into their weekly or monthly meetings and acknowledge people who uphold them. As we discussed above, leaders do well to think carefully about how intrinsic versus extrinsic they make the rewards or incentives that are provided for staff who reflect the organization's shared values. As well as reinforcing and acknowledging values-aligned behaviours across the organization, leaders can judiciously use these behaviours as the basis for more direct conversations with individuals who are not upholding these standards of behaviour. Leaders can very effectively use the organization's espoused values and behaviours as compass bearings or guides for these kinds of conversations. The values and behaviours provide a framework in which these conversations can happen, and actions agreed.

3. Using purpose to navigate complexity

A third challenge of leading with purpose relates to responding to complex issues and decisions. Leaders need to regularly make strategic decisions and navigate complex issues including conflicting agendas, priorities and personalities, much of which overrides, or at least significantly disrupts, formal lines of authority. Many of the complex decisions leaders and their teams make have clear, logical solutions that the group can arrive at, even if it takes time and lots of discussion to get there. However, some issues are knottier, especially those involving conflicting agendas, and priorities that cannot be easily reconciled with one another or are not easily identified. These challenges are often compounded in a work environment that is fast-paced, reactive and highly action-oriented. In these workplaces, the pace and energy preferences responding quickly, and often with technical solutions, rather than attentively and it doesn't work well with ambiguity and complexity.

Leading with purpose in these situations requires calmness and clarity. To an overloaded and stressed leader, engaging skilfully with purpose is a very difficult thing to do. When we're over-activated, our brain's amygdala within the limbic system kicks in and we switch into a kind of survival mode: the flight or fight response. The amygdala firing off is a huge help when we're in a house that's on fire, but it's not so useful when grappling with complexity and uncertainty, or sitting at our desk, leading a meeting or at 3 a.m. in bed. When we're overloaded, the brain's stress circuits overwhelm the executive functioning circuits (the leadership centres in the brain) that are meant to be processing information and making decisions. Research shows that we tend to make poorer decisions and perform significantly worse when cognitively overloaded or stressed in this way.[19] The emotional state of the leader can be every bit as contagious as an infectious virus. If staff catch the infection, they too bring this kind of scattered, frenetic energy to more complex or sensitive issues, often with disastrous consequences. Equally, if the leader can maintain calm amid chaos, clarity amid confusion or kindness amid criticism then that too can be infectious — in a good way.

The organization's purpose and values serve as a valuable compass in navigating a path forward, and in cutting through the frenzy of activity and mental busy-ness that often clouds these situations. Building alignment around how a course of action supports one or more of the organization's core values can be a powerful way of gaining buy-in and achieving resolution. Of course, this is not always the case. Sometimes, a course of action aligns with one core value (e.g. transparency) but conflicts with another (e.g. respect for privacy). But even making these conflicts explicit can help clarify the pros and cons of a particular course of action and what is at stake. It's about getting at the core value that each course of action supports. Here are some questions leaders can ask themselves in approaching these kinds of conflicted decisions.

Focus Question 7. How do our purpose and core values align with the different courses of action available to us in this situation? There will always be a range of factors to consider when working through complex issues and decisions. These might include alignment of values with strategy, the likely actions of key competitors and the impacts of the decision on different stakeholders (customers, shareholders, suppliers, staff, etc.). Sometimes these deliberations can get stuck, with parties unable to resolve conflicts between different possible courses of action. In these moments, bringing in the question of alignment with purpose and values can be powerful. This can help to cut through the noise and complexity and frame a set of options in a clearer light. Courses of action that do not align well with the organization's shared purpose and values ought not be worth pursuing. That is, assuming you have a clear and authentic purpose that reflects your organization's *actual* reason for being. Another way of asking the same question when considering a specific set of options, is: 'If we were to choose path A, how would we be reinforcing or undermining our purpose and core values? What about paths B and C?' A leadership team can go through each option on the table and consider it against these criteria. Oftentimes, an option will look attractive because it promises a short-term gain, but if it is counter to the essential purpose and values then it will nearly always lead to a much larger long-term loss. Having purpose and values up in 'headlights' when making more complex or contested decisions can be immensely valuable and can simplify the decision enormously. To the extent that the decision aligns with and reinforces and reflects the company's sense of purpose and values, you are strengthening them within the organization. From here, you then loop back to thinking about how the impacts of the decision will be communicated to those affected by it, including sharing the values that shaped how the decision was taken.

The leader's way: Authenticity

In the final section of this chapter, we focus on one fundamental leadership trait or attribute that we believe is core for embedding purpose within any organization. That is, *authenticity*. The word authenticity comes from the Ancient Greek, *authentikós* (αὐθεντικός), which means 'principal' or 'genuine'.[20] It implies a sense in which what is being presented is the genuine article or is what it says it is. A bit like buying gold jewellery and verifying that the piece is genuine. Another way of putting this is that when we are authentic, what we say we will do is reflected in what we actually do. Or what we say we feel or believe is actually what we feel or believe, and not what we feel pressured into thinking or feeling. Thus, the word is also derived from the Greek word *authentes*, which denotes 'self' and 'acting under one's own authority' as in self-mastery. Authenticity is about being true to ourselves and to others. It implies an alignment between our thoughts, our words and our actions.

We now explore how you, as a leader, can embody authenticity, and why this leadership trait matters for cultivating clear purpose. The following *practices* are all invaluable when trying to create a purpose-led organization. As with the previous *focus questions*, we offer these practices as areas for you to consider and reflect upon in your own leadership practice.

Practice 1: Do what you say you will do, and do not commit to things you know you cannot or will not do

This sounds easy but it takes discipline and awareness. It means that you are careful about what you promise but are reliable and predictable in delivering what you have committed to. It also means you have the courage to speak up and flag things you might be asked to deliver but will not be able to with the time and resources provided. In many ways, this is a hidden or undervalued leadership practice. Leaders rarely get promoted on the basis of this! And yet, this practice is absolutely fundamental to building a culture of honesty, respect and consistency. It is also foundational to building a culture based on ethical principles. When you think about it, there would be far fewer ethical scandals if leaders were able to live by this simple practice. So many ethical scandals and fractured professional relationships come from leaders papering over issues or behaviours that they know are not aligned with what the company or they personally have stated publicly. Whether it is the Wells Fargo scandal in the US, the Volkswagen scandal in Germany or the Evergrande scandal in China, this fundamental practice is missing in action in most of these situations. The nice thing about this practice, though, is that it applies at a much more day-to-day level, and you can implement it immediately. As a leader, you can embody this in all the small interactions and meetings you have with colleagues, day in, day out. This alignment and consistency in your behaviour sends a strong message to all around you and gives others the freedom to do the same.

Practice 2: Prioritize getting clear on your own values

Leading with authenticity requires clarity. Clarity on what is most important to you. A direct way of gaining clarity on what is important to you and how you want to lead is to reflect on values. Values are 'principles of action' that guide your responses and influence your decisions. Values are qualities of action that we can bring to the table. They are ways of working that we have a high level of control over. They are not emotions (which are how we feel) or goals (which are what we want). Our values are more like a compass bearing that tells us whether we're on course in terms of how we are leading others. They are not a destination we reach or a box we can tick. Examples of values that many leaders we work with might have include being honest and frank, being curious and questioning, showing empathy and compassion, thinking strategically and holistically, staying connected to others and prioritizing self-care.

Most people already know loosely what their values are, and mostly act in line with them. But few ever make them explicit. By making your values as a leader explicit, as well as your values in the other aspects of your life, you are gaining clarity on how you want to 'show up' in your leadership role. A bit like replacing an old camera lens with a new one, by making your values explicit, you are getting sharper resolution on how you want to be, and be seen, as a leader. You can also unpack any areas of alignment, as well as tension, between your values as a leader and the values you have for the other parts of your life (i.e. your personal values). Where there are big differences between your leadership and personal values, it is worth trying to understand what is driving these and how to resolve any potential conflict. Having identified your top three to four values, both leadership and personal, you then want to think about who you will share these with and how. As a leader, the more transparent and open you are about your leadership values, acknowledging that these are aspirational, the more you can build respect from those you lead. Assuming, of course, that you are upholding them enough so that your stated aspirations are credible — to both those you lead and yourself! We unpack these issues under Practices 3 and 4.

Practice 3: Speak openly and honestly

People are highly sensitive to any inconsistencies between what someone else says (or omits) and their underlying intentions, even if these perceptions are often wrong. Many, many research studies have highlighted this.[21,22] The more open and honest you can be as a leader with your team, the more respect you will earn and the more engagement and buy-in you will have. As discussed previously, this includes being open about what your values are as a leader. People will feel safer to share information, ideas, concerns and doubts. As a result, you will have better and richer information at hand and therefore will make better decisions. Better decisions equate to better performance and a more successful business. Speaking openly and honestly as a leader sends a powerful signal to those you lead that they can do the same. It creates an upward spiral of good conduct and healthy relationships. Being manipulative or deceitful also sends a powerful but not so healthy message. However, speaking openly and honestly takes confidence. It also takes courage at times, especially when you operate in an environment when your seniors do not work this way. In these cases, you need to navigate this carefully and decide whether this is really a personally or professionally healthy work environment for you to be in. To build a healthy habit, starting with small things and building up to bigger things, is the way to go. As you begin to see the benefits of interpersonal openness and honesty with your team, and that you're still respected by your seniors, the greater your confidence will be. The principle is simple: the more open and honest you can be with your team — even naming the issues or information you cannot share with your team, and why — the greater your team's confidence, engagement and performance will be.

Practice 4: Show vulnerability

A part of being authentic is to acknowledge our common humanity, and at times this includes acknowledging our vulnerability. This also relates to the above practice of speaking openly and honestly, but it focuses more on you, the leader, sharing your own personal challenges and even weaknesses. This can be a powerful practice tool and is an extension of Practice 3. Growing research evidence shows that when leaders do show vulnerability — even in relatively small ways — this adds to their authenticity. Even sharing more work-related things such as your own doubts or mistakes on a project (i.e. relatively 'safe' things) builds trust and engagement. Leaders can go further, too. When leaders share elements of their personal story, their challenges and 'crucible moments' (i.e. moments of great disorientation, change or loss), they create a sense of being human and 'normal'. This, in turn, creates a culture among the rest of the organization that allows people to feel safe bringing their 'whole self' to work. Again, it creates a virtuous cycle of authenticity. Our view, though, is that showing vulnerability should never be forced or pressured. Otherwise, it's suddenly inauthentic, it can backfire, and we've lost what we were reaching for.

Some points for reflection

Our suggestion is to consider how you are tracking against each of these practices of authenticity. On a scale of 1 to 10 (where 1 = not at all and 10 = in every action I take), you can ask yourself, to what extent am I living by each of these three practices? To what extent are these reflected in my leadership actions and decisions? What has been the cost of not acting in accord with these practices, or the benefit of acting in line with them? We can ask ourselves these questions honestly. We can also seek feedback (sometimes anonymous is best) from those we lead and our peers. How do those you lead rate you on these three behaviours on a scale from 1 to 10? Getting feedback on these practices can be hugely valuable, if not comforting and/ or surprising.

Another way of working with these practices is to keep a leadership journal and reflect daily or weekly on how you are tracking. By keeping regular track of your responses and behaviours, you build a 'picture' of how consistent you are on these practices — a bit like an anthropologist studying human behaviour, we can study ourselves! If you have a regular mindfulness practice, it will make this process of objectivity and self-awareness a lot easier and more fruitful. Or, if you have a trusted leadership coach, you could discuss each of these to better understand your challenges and what these practices mean for you in your role. Coaching is a great way of digging into these issues but in a confidential and constructive way.

Policy recommendations

Finally, we offer three policy recommendations for leaders to consider within an organization. These are designed to be organization-wide considerations for leaders and leadership teams.

» *Recommendation 1: Carve out time and resources to work on purpose.* Doing the work on keeping purpose fresh, relevant and practical takes time and resources. There are big advantages to planning and scheduling work that keeps purpose clear and tangible for people within the organization. This work needs to be built into the annual work cycle of the organization, and then embedded into more regular performance conversations.

» *Recommendation 2: Ensure that work on purpose is tied to the core strategic focus of the business.* This is not strictly a policy issue, but more a priority for the top leaders within any organization to ensure work on purpose is tied clearly to the core strategic business priorities of the company. The more connected and reinforcing work on purpose is with an organization's strategic priorities, the more likely it is to remain relevant and inform business decisions and behaviours. What you want to avoid is a purpose that is seen as being sugar coating for the company's *actual* purpose and reason for being. You are then pulling in two different directions, and your stated purpose will be ineffectual at best.

» *Recommendation 3: Embed conversations about purpose, values and high accountability within the performance and development structures of the organization.* Regular (e.g. quarterly) performance assessment and feedback conversations are the norm within almost every organization. Through these structured feedback sessions, you can create habits of providing and receiving feedback around purpose and values, as well as performance and delivery. Support staff in holding themselves, and one another, to account, via regular feedback, for the organization's values and purpose. This sends a powerful message to staff that questions of *how* we get our work done are as important as *what* we achieve.

Summary

In this chapter we have outlined some of the challenges of leading in an always-on work environment, and how this impacts leaders' capacity to lead with purpose. In an ever more distracted, frenetic environment, our view is that leaders need to be more conscious and deliberate, perhaps than ever before, about how and when they cultivate a clear sense of purpose within an organization. People's attention spans and bandwidth for these issues is increasingly limited and yet, these issues are more important than ever in keeping people clear on what their work contributes to and why it matters.

We have laid out a set of focus questions that leaders can consider in working out how you go about strengthening purpose within your team or organization. We also offer a core leadership 'trait', authenticity, that we believe is crucial to building a purpose-driven organization. As a part of this, we offered four practices that we believe strengthen any leaders' sense of authenticity. In the next chapter, Priorities, we move to unpack the challenges leaders face in setting priorities and staying focused in an always-on environment. Again, we highlight key leadership challenges that relate to setting priorities, and that are especially impacted by the always-on workplace. We will offer a further set of focus questions and core leadership practices to help address these challenges.

Chapter 3

Priorities

We've considered some of the issues related to purpose, so now let's consider a number of questions related to priorities. What are your priorities as a leader? Are they what you assume they are? Are they what they should be? How does my team or wider organization set priorities? Who or what is setting your priorities? Do you need to reflect on and reset your priorities?

Gaining clarity on what is most critical (i.e. your priorities) and then keeping yourself and your people focused on them is among the most important and challenging things a leader does. Yet, in an age of info-whelm and distraction, this core capacity can easily be degraded. In this chapter, we explore some of the challenges with prioritizing in the always-on world. We also provide a series of practical exercises or experiments which can shed light on what is going on and what you can do about it.

Drinking from the fire hose

Ravi is a middle-level manager and highly committed to his occupation. He wants to progress in his career, works long hours, rarely takes breaks, eats lunch at his desk most days and cares a lot about the organization and the people in it. Nevertheless, despite feeling that he is always on the go, Ravi has a niggling feeling that he doesn't achieve as much in his working day and life as he should. While his day is filled with reacting to seemingly urgent priorities that are, perhaps, not that important, the in-box is forever full of important but non-urgent priorities that always seem to be on the backburner.

One day, Ravi was walking through the kitchen at home where his ten-year-old son was building a model airplane on the kitchen table. Ravi's son looked up and asked him, 'All the kids at school were talking about what their parents do at work. I said you were a businessman, but I didn't really know what that meant. So, what do you do at work, Dad?' Ravi paused a moment and said, 'I answer emails and Slack messages — that's my work.' Unimpressed, his son shrugged his shoulders and turned back to making his model. This was a turning point for Ravi.

Since Stephen Covey wrote his bestselling book *First Things First*,[1] the problem of balancing the important versus not important, and the urgent versus not urgent, has become harder, not easier. As we explored in Chapter 1, the rise of information technology is meant to make life easier, not harder. But as the consultancy firm Bain and Company noted:

> *By our estimates, a senior executive who in the 1970s might have received fewer than 1000 outside phone calls, telexes or telegrams a year now faces a tidal wave of 30,000 emails and other electronic communications.*[2]

To make the matter worse, now we also have all sorts of internal messaging systems that have taken this torrent of information to the next level. According to Rani Molla:

> *On average, employees at large companies are each sending more than 200 Slack messages per week... Keeping up with these conversations can seem like a full-time job. After a while, the software goes from helping you work to making it impossible to get work done.*[3]

Deluged by such messages, often from multiple platforms, the priority subtly but surely shifts from getting the work done that we thought we were there to do to just keeping on top of the flood of so-called 'work' appearing in a variety of inboxes. As technology gets faster and more ubiquitous, we are being fed a never-ending and fast-flowing stream of information, like we are trying to drink it from a fire hose. Surveys suggest that employees only spend, at best, 45 per cent of their time working on what they are primarily employed to do.[4] The rest of the time is spent on 'busywork' like emails, meetings, bureaucracy, administrative tasks and unplanned interruptions. And, the way we are going, the situation is only getting worse.

The servant becomes the master

This constant flow of information, however, would not be so much of a problem if we were able to turn it off, or at least turn it down, but most of us aren't doing that either because we can't or don't want to. Technology is meant to be a servant and we its master, but many leaders have been conditioned to think that busywork is more important than it is, or workplaces have created systems that require it of us. Others are addicted to the constant demands of technology, which is not surprising considering that it is designed to be addictive.[5] As former Facebook executive Chamath Palihapitiya said in an interview: 'The short-term dopamine-driven feedback loops that we have created are destroying how society works.'[6]

These dopamine circuits are otherwise known as the brain's reward networks, in that they give the brain a little burst of 'pleasure' in the form of a dopamine-hit whenever we do something to trigger it. Eating, for example, is pleasurable because we need to do it to survive, but in the case of overeating, the brain's pleasure centre — rather than the executive functioning centre — is making the decision. The former works on 'wants' and the latter works on 'needs'. Hence, we overeat and get sick as a result. The same networks are implicated when you receive a notification on your phone or a 'like' on social media. These days they are getting stimulated all the time. Soon we are driven to do more and more of the thing that triggers the pleasure response to get the same pleasure-hit. The sting in the tail, however, is that what starts out as seeking those little pleasure-hits in the reward circuits of the brain soon evolves into a retreat from the anxiety and pain associated with not having them. The brain begins by whispering, then calling, until it screams out for 'satisfaction'. That's what addiction is all about — we experience pain if we try to withdraw from the thing we have become addicted to. Soon we don't have much control over the behaviour, and the object of our addiction is the master and we are its servant. It's a little like a dog walking along not knowing it's on a leash until it pulls against it, then it realizes it's not its own master any longer.

The things we become addicted to, or conditioned by, become our priorities whether they deserve it or not. As long as we have constant access to the object of our craving (and we haven't experienced any problems associated with pursuing the addiction at the expense of other important things), then we don't see what the problem is. It doesn't mean there isn't a problem, but just that we haven't noticed it yet. The behaviour goes on in the shadows until one of two problems arise. First, we don't have the ability to satisfy our craving (e.g. you lost or broke your smartphone) in which case we experience the pain, anxiety, confusion and agitation of withdrawal. Alternatively, we single-mindedly pursue the object of our addiction but in the process sacrifice other things required to keep us healthy (e.g. relationships, exercise, sleep or leisure activities).

> **Practical experiment 1: How addicted to your technology are you?**
>
> You might like to try the following experiment, especially if you aren't sure whether you are addicted to your device. Try having a day totally without it — that means not even having it on your person. If you feel fine then it's not likely you are addicted. If you don't feel fine and you can't get your mind away from thinking about it or you feel compelled to pick it up, then you probably are addicted and might do well to start weaning yourself off it.

Too much on my mind

The effect of the modern work environment on people's attention and behaviour was named some time ago in an article in the *Harvard Business Review*. It was described as a newly recognized neurological phenomenon: attention deficit trait or ADT.[7] ADT is a bit like driving a car and forgetting where the brake pedal is because you are so busy thinking about something else. It's a common response to a hyperkinetic, time-pressured environment where trying to deal with too much input results in secondary effects including black-and-white thinking, difficulty staying organized, setting priorities, managing time and a constant low level of panic and guilt. Sometimes, when people are introduced to mindfulness, the results of ADT become glaringly apparent, revealing indicators such as stress, impatience, motor restlessness and distractibility. It would be easy to think that the mindfulness practice wasn't working when in fact it was doing its job — showing us what is going on under the surface and what we are oblivious to most of the time.

One of the first effects of being 'always on' and overloading the brain with information is that it creates a high cognitive or mental load. This mental overload has various flow-on effects. First, it diminishes our ability to focus or pay attention. Microsoft Canada reported in 2015 that the average person's attention span had dropped from 12 seconds to 8 seconds between 2000 and 2015 (apparently, that's now less than a goldfish).[8] Twelve seconds wasn't particularly good to start with, but eight seconds?

Practical experiment 2: Test your attention span

If you're not sure how long your attention span is, try sitting quietly for five minutes and pay attention to nothing other than the sensation of the breath entering and leaving the nose. Notice how often the mind wanders off into 'thinking' mode even if that thinking is about questions such as, 'Why am I doing this?' or 'Am I being mindful?'

Degraded attention negatively impacts performance which can manifest itself in many ways. For example, in the US, it is estimated that over 250,000 people die each year as a result of medical errors, making it the third largest cause of death in that country.[9] In Australia, distracted driving, largely due to the misuse of technology, has become a more significant cause of major road accidents than drink driving.[10]

Whether in hospitals or on the roads, reducing errors is a major priority, but what are some of the factors that increase errors? A study on university students got them to complete a simple task while their performance, including their error rate, was tracked.[11] Then, on the second run through, they were split into three groups where, unbeknown to them, they would either get a call on their phone, receive a text message or not be interrupted. Receiving phone calls led to a 28 per cent increase in mistakes despite the fact that the students' phones had been set to vibrate and they were instructed not to take them out or look at them while being tested. Another study showed that just having the phone within eyesight, even if it was turned off and face down, was enough to significantly reduce performance on a whole range of executive functions.[12] Furthermore, the more a person tended to use their phone in daily life the larger the impact was. It's like 10–20 IQ points gone — boom! That's not even considering the effect it has on the EQ scale. More of that in Chapter 4, 'People'.

One of the key problems with the excessive volume of information we face is that, unless we control the inputs well, we experience a very high cognitive load and our mind cannot fulfil its functions well. To use an analogy, the mind is like a room where we need to get jobs done. High cognitive load is like a room with way too much stuff in it to be useful. The room can't fulfil its functions — it becomes dysfunctional.

High cognitive load has also been found to significantly reduce creativity and lead to short-cut, automatic pilot, predictable responses.[13] Another study examined whether doing a secondary executive task interfered with the quality of decision-making relating to calculated risks while gambling.[14] Doing two executive tasks is a bit like scanning your email inbox for important emails while at the same time trying to make decisions. The study found that if participants had two executive tasks running simultaneously then they made poorer decisions than those who were only doing the one task of making decisions. Those poorer, riskier decisions cost them. As the adage goes: just do one job at a time. The overloaded mind can't process the volume of information coming at it and attempts to take shortcuts just to reduce the load and avoid working too hard. This is a profound shift in priorities from doing a job well to mere survival.

Professor Ron Epstein is a senior physician, researcher and academic with a strong interest in mindful practice. He shares examples from his and other physicians' experience where the temptation to decide a course of action in a complex clinical situation is profoundly different depending on whether it presents itself in the middle of the night compared to during the day. During a long overnight shift the fatigued mind will tend to want to take the easiest course of action and convince itself that the situation doesn't need further complex investigations. The same clinical signs presenting during the day generally will lead to doing these further tests. The fatigued, overloaded mind wants to take the easiest and shortest path and convince itself it is certain of what's going on even when it's not. The less fatigued and more alert mind will just get on with what is necessary.

We are seeing the same impacts with information overload. When leaders are controlled by the environment and find themselves in a hyper-reactive mode, prioritizing and making good decisions becomes much more difficult. When we are over-activated, stressed and fatigued, our brain struggles to recruit the core executive functions needed to prioritize and respond strategically. The flight or fight response overwhelms our brain's executive function networks, meaning we're more prone to black-and-white decision making, and an inability to see problems from multiple angles.[15] We end up sucked into problems and conflicts based more on emotional reactivity than on strategic sense.

Black-and-white thinking is another example of where the fatigued mind just wants to take the shortest route to any answer, whether or not it is the best answer or takes account of complexity. For leaders, this means our own and our team's resources are diverted from strategically valuable priorities — or even taking the time to set a clear strategy in the first place! Sometimes, this can create a vicious cycle, where one poor decision leads to several other 'fires' that then require several more difficult decisions, which, when overloaded, are also made poorly, or take significant resources to turn around.

If you practise something like a mindfulness exercise, the chances are that you will notice your mind buzzing and fidgeting and the attention jumping to anything that moves. It is therefore very useful to have strategies to reduce cognitive load and to help the mind refresh itself and stabilise attention.

Practical experiment 3: Keep simple moments simple

We often overthink things in life and at work. You might therefore like to experiment with keeping simple moments simple throughout the day. Stay in the moment. So, for example, if you have a two-minute walk to a meeting or a presentation, just walk with an awareness of the body moving, rather than walking on automatic pilot while the attention is habitually feeding worries. Give yourself two minutes of mental rest and a chance of cultivating a calmer, more attentive state of mind. If you're making a cup of tea, just make the tea, rather than scrolling your phone while you make the tea. If you're driving, just attend to the driving, don't listen to the radio or a podcast.

The unstrategic leader

The degrading of our attention outlined above also has impacts at a more 'macro' level, in the form of leadership strategy. When we are cognitively overloaded, we are much less likely to be able to think strategically. In his recent book *The Crux*, Richard

Rumelt, a world-leading researcher and thinker on business strategy, argues that being able to step back and identify a small set (e.g. three or four) of the company's most difficult but surmountable challenges, is the core of what it means to be a strategic leader. Rumelt calls this 'challenge-based strategy'. It sounds very simple, and on paper, it is. But in practice, it's a difficult thing to do.[16] One reason that challenge-based strategy is so difficult is that many shareholders, executives and boards are simply not interested in tackling the more complex, risky problems because of the costs of failure (even with the possibility of groundbreaking innovation).

Rumelt's more significant point, though, is that many CEOs and business leaders simply do not know *how* to think about strategic challenges in a productive, direct and robust way. They lack the 'bandwidth' to be able to step right back and think deeply and honestly about where they are in the industry, and what forces are holding them back. While there are, doubtless, rational bases for not taking risks, Rumelt points to the inner mindsets that often hold leaders back from at least engaging with the more complex challenges a business faces. In our view, cognitive overload, mental fatigue and information overwhelm are only going to amplify this challenge. When cognitively stretched, leaders are far less likely to be able to — let alone *want* to — engage in the tough, strategic thinking and prioritizing of strategic leadership. Engaging in strategic leadership takes a kind of mental clarity and interpersonal honesty and confidence that do not thrive in someone who is overloaded and overwhelmed.

Focus Question 1: How well do I engage in strategic leadership and what role does mental fatigue and overload play in this? Take 15 minutes to reflect on your leadership role. How much time and attention do you give to thinking strategically about your business or team's priorities? How have you built strategic thinking into your weekly, monthly or annual schedule? As a leader, you want to be regularly checking in on, and refreshing, your strategic priorities. Also consider the kinds of blockages and barriers that exist to you taking time out, perhaps with your senior leadership team, for honest strategic reflection and prioritizing. Is there anything you need to do within your leadership team so that you prioritize regular time for strategic reflection and have the bandwidth to engage fully with it when you do? What supports do your senior leadership team need to feel less overloaded and mentally clear enough to engage with this kind of thinking? Just making this a priority generally doesn't work, as it just adds to a sense of overload and overwhelm. Instead, nutting out which issues or tasks you should drop or delegate to someone else, and how you will do this, can be an effective way of creating space for this all-important strategic work.

Acting politically

In addition to the need to think strategically, effective leaders also need to act politically. By 'acting politically', we do not mean unbridled Machiavellianism, manipulation and deceit. These behaviours are never productive of a thriving, successful organization. Instead, we mean a kind of situational awareness that is attuned to the power dynamics in which you operate. That is, the people and networks which exist in your environment that hold power and have influence. In almost every organization, many of these centres of power and influence will not be tied to a specific role. They can also be tied to particular individuals or groups who have expertise, their own connections, or experience within the organization that is not entirely linked to their formal role. Understanding and working with these power dynamics is crucial to having influence and getting things done. It's a bit like navigating a route through a forest to a campsite. Your compass will tell you which direction you need to head to reach your campsite. But it won't tell you where the rivers, cliffs or ridge lines are along the way. For this, you need the map. You use the map to avoid the cliffs and rivers, as well as take advantage of the ridge lines. Political awareness is a bit like the map.

As leaders, when we are attentionally stretched and overloaded, we tend to put the map down. Following the direction of the compass is much easier and simpler. A bit like the black-and-white thinking and reactivity that we have when we are mentally overloaded, our political awareness can easily suffer. Cognitively, we struggle to accommodate the complexity and nuance of navigating power dynamics and instead resort to technical, linear solutions to problems. Technical solutions are far less demanding. But invariably these fail. If we have not factored in and considered the political dynamics of the environment in which we operate, we end up in a river or off the edge of a cliff.

The groundbreaking work of Ron Heifetz and Martin Linsky in their writing and research of leadership models describes these dynamics beautifully. In their work on adaptive leadership, Heifetz and Linsky distinguish technical from adaptive challenges. Technical challenges are those where existing authority structures and expertise can solve the problem, where established patterns of working and operating procedures are useful, and where the solution is identifiable and feasible. The analogy Heifetz and Linsky use is open heart surgery. Although a highly complex procedure involving multiple highly skilled and well-trained individuals, there is a standard approach to open heart surgery that will, almost always, succeed. Adaptive challenges on the other hand, lack a clearly defined solution or set of solutions, do not have an established operating procedure for resolving them, and are not addressable within the established authority structures that exist. Adaptive challenges are much harder to diagnose, and harder still to address. An example Heifetz and Linsky use to describe adaptive challenges is how do you prevent the heart surgery patient from returning to McDonald's after the surgery? This is a far tougher problem.

Most leadership challenges are more adaptive than technical. A core part of why this is the case is because of the political environment in which most leaders exist. As Heifetz and Linsky argue, this is why most change initiatives fail. Leaders of change initiatives often make the mistake of treating an adaptive challenge as if it were a technical one.

Focus Question 2: How effective am I at diagnosing and addressing adaptive challenges? Take 15 minutes to map out one important initiative you have led or contributed to over the past couple of years. To what extent was this initiative an adaptive challenge? That is, to what extent was:

1. the crux of the challenge difficult to diagnose?
2. a clear solution not easily identifiable?
3. established sources of authority (e.g. leaders/individuals in positions of formal authority) unable to address the problem?
4. established operating procedures (e.g. established accountabilities and ways of working within the organization) unable to deliver on the initiative?

Reflect on how you approached the project. To what extent did you and your colleagues treat it as if it were a technical challenge? What were the impacts of this? Now reflect on a challenge or initiative you are currently planning or working on. To what extent are you treating this project as an adaptive challenge? Are there any changes you might need to make so you are treating the more adaptive elements of the project as adaptive? What are the rivers and cliff lines for your project? What are the ridge lines? How attuned is your political antenna? Are there any conversations you might need to have to ensure your initiative is a success?

Distraction, discernment and decision making

Having explored the challenge of leading strategically and politically, we now consider the related but more specific issues of leadership decision making and distraction. When overloaded, we tend to default to more energy-efficient ways of working, which, as we've discussed, tend to undermine the strategic and political astuteness of our actions. But when we can step back, assess the strategic and political dynamics we face and identify a course of action, the next challenge becomes how to stay on track. Returning to the compass and map analogy, the map is critical for knowing the terrain we're in and what lies ahead. But once we start on our journey through the forest, we need to stay on track. We need to stay disciplined and not fall prey to the temptation to take shortcuts that will very likely get us badly lost.

A core leadership skill for staying on track is being able to set priorities well, and to stick to them. In the information age, there is literally a deluge of potential diversions and distractions that leaders face. Often, these distractions are dressed up as urgencies. The key challenge for the leader is how to discern the important from the unimportant, using both political awareness and strategic clarity, to make these decisions. To do this well, we need to be present and awake. We need to prioritize.

The research shows us that setting priorities and realizing them requires three core skills: first, attention; then discernment; and lastly, decision. Attention is necessary for seeing the situation and information in front of us. Then we need to discern what we see, sifting what is most from what is least relevant. The final step is to decide on an advantageous way forward (optimizing beneficial outcomes) based on what we have in front of us. This whole decision-making process can be undermined if the required precondition of attention is undermined by distraction.

If anything, distractibility has got worse in recent years, not better. A review of psychological, psychiatric and neuroimaging research demonstrated how the Internet seems to be changing our cognitive abilities for the worse.[17] This review identified three executive functions and their corresponding brain regions that don't seem to be functioning particularly well in the modern day. These relate to attentional capacities, memory, and social and emotional intelligence. Attention diminishes when many incoming sources of information and notifications constantly divide attention and wrench it from one thing to another. Memory suffers because there is little need to use it when all information can be stored on our devices or googled rather than being remembered. If we don't 'exercise' brain circuits throughout life they waste away through disuse, which does not augur well for later life. Social and emotional intelligence suffers because real interactions with other humans are increasingly being replaced by virtual ones.

Professor Amishi Jha is a neuroscientist with a strong interest in how we manage attention. She has worked extensively with leaders in the US military to help leaders and soldiers to not only manage stress but to also make better decisions.[18] She was struck by the fact that the pre-deployment training of soldiers degraded their attention (i.e. their training made attention worse, not better). It should be the other way around — training should improve attention. Hence the need to train attention as a central objective of overall military training.[19] Professor Jha uses the acronym VUCA (see Table 1) to describe the environment many leaders operate in, and which can 'degrade' attention if not managed well. [20] VUCA stands for the factors of volatility, uncertainty, complexity and ambiguity.

Table 1: Things that degrade attention

V	Volatility
U	Uncertainty
C	Complexity
A	Ambiguity

In such situations we tend to feel stressed and/or uncomfortable and we try to alleviate our suffering by taking mental shortcuts and clutching onto anything we see as certain, simple and unambiguous, whether it is or not. We can, of course, minimize the impact of VUCA with strategies such as being better able to manage stress, feeling more comfortable with uncertainty and ambiguity, and training attention through mindfulness.

Things that degrade attention can be looked at in another way. As lovers of alliteration, we like to think of them as the three Es (see Table 2). These stand for Environment, Emotional state and Errant practices.

Table 2: Three Es

Environment	Distracting, volatile, uncertain, complex, ambiguous
Emotional state	Stress, anger, fear
Errant practices	Cognitive overload
	Interrupting the flow
	Misuse of technology
	Complex multitasking

Consider the impact of the environments within which we live and work. The traditional library is a carefully designed environment to make concentration and deep engagement easy — studious, quiet, little movement and partitioned reading desks. A casino is a carefully designed environment replete with subtle conditioned stimuli and elements to foster the mental torpor required to keep mindlessly gambling. The open-plan office, although designed ostensibly to be laid-back and innovative, is very different. A review of over 100 studies explored the impact of different office environments on wellbeing and performance.[21] It showed that open-plan offices actually diminish attention spans, productivity, creativity and work satisfaction, mostly due to uncontrolled interactions, higher stress and lower motivation.

Our emotional state, whether it be that of the individual or group, can have an enormous impact on attention. Emotions like stress, anger, fear and panic are contagious and, in such states, certain things are fixated upon, regardless of their actual threat or importance, to the exclusion of other perhaps more important things. This has an immediate and profound impact upon priorities. Hans Rosling worked for many years with the World Health Organization and various government organizations around the world. He was a master of collecting big data and using it to make informed, rational and effective decisions in highly complex situations. In his fascinating, deeply insightful book, *Factfulness*, Rosling gives numerous examples of where this is done well and poorly.[22] One chapter called 'The Urgency Instinct' deals with the impact of the emotional state on decisions. For example, when someone wants you to make a poor decision — perhaps buying something you can't afford and won't suit your needs — they will often foster a sense of urgency or fear in you to make you act impulsively and not do your due diligence. We don't have the space to go into some of the contemporary issues where this sense of fear and urgency is being strategically and systematically used to compel action, but a cool head, good data and an impartial and objective attitude are required lest the impulsive solutions we implement waste enormous amounts of resources and, in the process, make the problem worse rather than better. For example, take an issue such as dealing with climate change. This needs action, but if fear and urgency rule, then we may make policy decisions and take actions that are wasteful, not sustainable and cost far more than the benefits they deliver. Time will tell.

The third E stands for errant practices. A couple of these practices — such as interrupting the flow and complex multitasking — are listed in Table 1 and have been previously discussed. Subsequent studies have replicated this basic finding: trying to stretch our attention across too much information simultaneously undermines our cognitive performance (e.g. poor memory, impaired decision making, higher stress, increased errors, poor communication). For example, a recent study of US knowledge workers found that when employees used email or other text communication to solve complex problems, it undermined their performance not just on the task at hand, but also on subsequent complex or ambiguous work tasks.[23] It appears that using tech-enabled communication to engage with complex problems generates a cognitive deficit that spills over and hurts our capacity to use our important executive functions for other tasks. Having the flow of complex tasks interrupted by a secondary task has a number of negative impacts as well, including losing time. Probably about a day a week of lost productivity is due to this errant practice.[24] This is also when errors are often made.

This misuse and overuse of technology is becoming a bigger problem, especially for younger employees who have habituated themselves to this way of studying, living and working since childhood. It promises a fuller, more productive life but delivers the exact opposite. Hence, an effective leader doesn't just need to manage their own attention well, they also need to foster the environment, emotional state and work practices that will help others to manage theirs.

There are various reasons why things like distraction, stress, urgency and high cognitive load impair leaders' decision-making abilities. One reason is attentional, another is emotional and a third is psychological. The attentional distortion relates to partial or selective attention. When rushed or overloaded we tend to fixate on or become hypervigilant about some things but blind to others that may be staring us in the face. We either can't, or don't want to, see them. The attention narrows down and we find it difficult to pan back to see the big picture.

Emotions, while they can be energizing and highly motivating, can also mislead us. When the emotional state tips into urgency, fear or stress, then the brain's stress circuits amplify the fixation of attention on some things to the exclusion of others. Furthermore, the over-activation of the amygdala impairs the executive functioning circuits that are meant to be weighing priorities, assessing data and determining a measured response. When stressed in this way, we will tend to flail around and over- or under-react. The high cognitive load, through mental fatigue, predisposes the mind to want to take the shortest route to any old decision, whether it is a good one or not.

Mindfully decluttering the room

Having considered the above, we are left with some fundamental *focus questions* to help us work towards effective and targeted solutions.

Focus Question 3: What do I need to do about this? Focusing on problems without solutions can be very demotivating and demoralizing. As we have previously mentioned, the mind is like a room and it is a lot less functional when it is cluttered and dark. To function better, it needs decluttering and to let in more light. How do we do this? One solution that is increasingly used to good effect in many workplaces is mindfulness. Mindfulness involves increasing present moment awareness; it is the equivalent of letting in light. Then, because we are just paying attention to one thing at any given moment, and not worrying about 1000 things related to the future or the past, we can reduce the mental load or clutter. We can keep simple moments simple. If we are walking, then just walk, not walk *and* worry. If we are working towards a tight deadline, then just work, not work *and* worry.

Focus Question 4: What are the benefits of increasing awareness? When cognitive load is reduced, say through the practice of mindfulness, then leaders can, among other things, enhance creativity. There are two main types of mindfulness meditation practice: focused attention and open monitoring. Focusing attention is like concentration and open monitoring is like being impartially aware of whatever comes into the field of awareness. To use a metaphor, focused attention is like the light projected from a torch, and open monitoring is like the light coming from a light globe hanging from the ceiling. Interestingly, it seems that these two main types of mindfulness practice have different effects on the two main aspects of the creative process — convergent and divergent thinking. Divergent thinking is like brainstorming, where you have an open mind and allow various possibilities to arise. One idea may stand out in which case you choose that idea to take further. Convergent thinking is focusing on that idea, planning it out and bringing it to fruition. Focused attention, it seems, particularly enhances convergent thinking, and open monitoring enhances divergent thinking.[25]

Mindfulness has been found to provide a range of other benefits. For example, one study we were involved with measured the impact of an eight-week mindfulness program on university administrative and academic staff.[26] We measured a range of parameters pre-program, post-program and then six months later. Our key findings included improvements in self-rated performance, wellbeing, eudaemonic wellbeing (meaningfulness), work engagement (particularly vigour and dedication), authenticity (self-awareness, authentic behaviour, open relationships) and satisfaction with life. Importantly, these improvements were sustained at the six-month follow-up.

Focus Question 5: Is it just about the leader? The leader is a central figure for establishing workplace culture, attitudes and practices for team members, so increasing the abilities and qualities described above is a significant investment in the team's wellbeing and capacities. Research has shown that a leader, just by virtue of being more mindful, has the effect of improved employee performance and work–life balance in their employees. It is also associated with less emotional exhaustion and less tendency to deviate from instructions and sound policy.[27] A leader's level of mindfulness also buffers the relationship between emotional exhaustion (a key component of burnout) and negative mood and poor behaviour (i.e. mindfulness helps the situation not to spiral into poor mood and abusive supervision).[28] Of course, if there are systemic and workplace culture issues that need to be addressed, then just teaching people to be mindful in order to tolerate it better will be a superficial solution and will likely diminish the impetus required to make necessary changes.

Meaning, mindfulness, motivation and metacognition

Recently there has been a lot of interest in mindfulness' potential to increase meaning. One group proposed the term 'Mindfulness to Meaning Theory (MMT)'[29] which is based on a synthesis of research and experience. MMT emphasizes the importance of a person's ability to 'decentre' or objectively stand back from the thinking mind and its appraisals of situations as being inherently stressful. This ability to stand back from the mind and its contents (thoughts and emotions) is called metacognition. Metacognitive ability is linked to better mental health[30] but it also protects us from a range of other problems. It helps people to cultivate eudaemonic meaning in the face of adversity and facilitates a more adaptive and flexible reappraisal of stressful situations. One might, for example, look at adversity or an error of judgment not so much as a negative event that one continues to regret and criticize but more as a valuable opportunity to reinforce a lesson. The former leads to a continuing negative affect producing nothing good in return whereas the latter leads to meaning, insight and more discerning decisions in the future.

The Dunning–Kruger effect

One important benefit of metacognitive ability is that it helps to protect people from the so-called 'Dunning–Kruger effect' which is the common phenomenon of people holding overly favourable views of their actual abilities.[31] An unskilled person — whether they be a leader or team member — is then vulnerable to suffering the dual burdens of not only coming to erroneous conclusions and making unfortunate choices but also being robbed of the metacognitive ability to realize their incompetence. As a result, the person is resistant to being corrected unless they develop the self-awareness and objectivity required to form a more accurate assessment of their performance. Paradoxically, improving people's skills and metacognitive competence helps them recognize their limitations and be more open to feedback. Therefore, the astute leader is less likely to tell people that their performance is poor — although they may need to do that sometimes — but is more invested in giving people the tools they need to be able to see it for themselves. The former often leads to resentment but the latter often leads to gratitude.

Greater metacognition results in a broader and more contextual state of attention and a wider ability to be open to novel information and different perspectives. This, in turn, provides the potential for better mental flexibility, problem solving and reappraisal of the situations one finds oneself in.[32] With this greater awareness, flexibility and discernment, it is common for people to choose to be motivated by deeper or intrinsic values.

These, in turn, inform behaviours and thus engender greater meaning in life (eudaemonia).

Cognitive biases

Another important quality that the best leaders have is the ability to make less biased decisions. There are two broad categories of bias — conscious and unconscious. Unconscious bias operates below a person's level of awareness whereas a conscious bias is one that a person is aware of. We can't do much about unconscious bias unless someone or something brings it to our attention. In the absence of awareness, an unconscious bias will operate and affect how we think, behave and judge people and situations. It distorts what we do see and blinds us to other things. There are also many kinds of individual biases that have been described, such as *confirmation* bias (i.e. pursuit of data that supports a view over data that refutes it), *anchoring* bias (i.e. resistance to adapting appropriately to subsequent data that suggests an alternative view), and *availability* bias (i.e. the tendency to think that examples of things that come readily to mind are more representative than is actually the case). It is becoming increasingly clear that people who are more self-aware are less affected by these cognitive biases, which helps them to appraise a situation more accurately and to make better decisions.[33] It's not so much that a person who is innately more mindful, or trains themselves in mindfulness, doesn't have biases — we're all human — but that the more mindful a person is the better able they are to spot biases when they arise. This means being less likely to unconsciously jump to conclusions and more likely to keep attention and mind open to receive incoming information.

Evidence from Hafenbrack and colleagues suggests that being more mindful is associated with being less affected by various forms of cognitive bias such as sunk-cost bias. This is defined as the 'tendency to continue an endeavour once an investment in money, effort or time has been made.'[34] We may keep going with a line of action or a decision even when it's clear that it is unwise to do so and that we should step away. Large-scale examples include disastrous military campaigns, over-budget projects or an overly rapid expansion of a business. Small-scale and personal examples could include not selling declining stock, ignoring bad advice that has been paid for, staying too long in a dysfunctional relationship or job, or adding to a gambling debt by gambling more. Sunk-cost bias is attenuated by mindfulness for two main reasons: it draws focus away from the past to focus on the present (i.e. to be able to read the writing on the wall), and it reduces negative mood principally through detachment (i.e. just let it go). This is not giving up — it is about making a better choice. An indication that it is a mindful decision will be the sense of release and unburdening after it is made.

Acting ethically

There are many competing priorities for leaders. For example, the drive to increase output, make profits and climb the promotional ladder can clash with the innate desire to be fair to others or act ethically. Many unethical decisions stem from a lack of awareness as a result of being on automatic pilot and fixated by some secondary reward (e.g. making money or getting ahead). A series of studies[35] showed that individuals high in mindfulness were more likely to act ethically, value upholding ethical standards, and to inform their decision making by a principled approach. More mindful leaders place greater intrinsic value on their moral identity and not just on the secondary gains they anticipate getting. The other valuable aspect of awareness is that we are more able to notice the effect of acting against our conscience or deeper values — it is stressful and it doesn't give us peace of mind. In such situations, the mind is often active in making justifications and the fear of being caught out. These are tell-tale signs and if we recognize them early enough we can turn back.

Mental health, motivation and productivity

Some people see mindfulness as simply a 'relaxation' exercise or just a way to help tolerate distress. Yes, it has been shown to improve workplace wellbeing and mental health.[36] Yes, it has been found to significantly reduce emotional exhaustion and increase job satisfaction.[37] Yes, leaders' ability to be more mindful more often is positively associated with different facets of employee wellbeing, such as job satisfaction, need satisfaction, and different dimensions of employee performance, such as in-role performance and organizational citizenship behaviours.[38,39] But, although people higher in mindfulness are less likely to feel frustration, even in unsupportive managerial environments we should be wary of workplace-based mindfulness interventions being provided to improve employees' ability to cope without addressing underlying problems in workplace culture and practices.[40] The individual is not separate from the collective. The tokenistic and perhaps strategic introduction of mindfulness for employees to make them more productive but without addressing the dysfunctional work environment that may be causing the problems in the first place is sometimes called McMindfulness.[41]

But do productivity and wellbeing run in parallel or are they competitors? That depends. Feeling more relaxed is a common side effect of being in the present moment because one is less anxious about outcomes, but many high-performing individuals driven by output, KPIs and the like see mindfulness as undesirable and counterproductive because 'relaxed' is synonymous with 'unmotivated'. An interesting study tested this idea.[42] Sure enough, they found that doing mindfulness-based practices was associated with lower motivation. But, paradoxically, it also led to higher performance. That doesn't initially make sense because we try to motivate ourselves or others in order to perform better. However, it does make sense if you look at the common assumptions about motivation and how it is measured, and then how mindfulness is related to performance.

Motivation is most often measured according to two criteria — arousal and future focus. Arousal is another way of saying stress — you stress people by putting them under pressure and you assume that they will perform better than if they were relaxed (i.e. apathetic and not engaged with the task). Future focus means that the person is concerned about the outcome or result of the task (i.e. will I win, will it be good enough, will I get a bonus?). What does mindfulness do? It helps a person to be calmer (less arousal) and to take the focus off the outcome by focusing more on the work at hand. Less future focus means more focus on the present moment process. By the assumed motivational metric, that is less motivation but, in reality, it is just a matter of not needing to be motivated by stress and worry about the outcome. Performing better is the result of being more focused on the task. Being less stressed is the result of being less anxious about the outcome, which often distracts a person from the process. That is a win-win situation.

Other evidence shows us that mindfulness is of central importance in determining our priorities and ability to deal with action crises. Action crises are defined as the 'conflicts people face when deciding whether to continue pursuing or to give up a goal for which difficulties keep arising.'[43] Research shows that greater mindfulness predicts fewer action crises for two main reasons; firstly, due to people being more connected to their intrinsic goal motivation rather than being driven by external rewards and, secondly, people have a greater ability to handle difficult emotions during challenging times without being overwhelmed by them.

Another study explored how intrinsic or extrinsic aspirations related to goal attainment and wellbeing.[44] Unsurprisingly, both intrinsic and extrinsic motivation led to greater goal attainment but, perhaps surprisingly, they were far different in their effect on wellbeing. Attainment of intrinsic aspirations (e.g. personal growth, close relationships, community involvement and physical health) related positively to wellbeing (i.e. life satisfaction, self-esteem and positive mood), which was largely due to its impact on the satisfaction of psychological needs such as autonomy, competence and relatedness. Attainment of extrinsic aspirations on the other hand (e.g. money, fame and image) was strongly related to 'illbeing' (i.e. anxiety, physical symptoms and negative mood).

Focus Question 6: What are you really motivated by? Take some time to reflect on what motivates your actions. Are you driven by stress and future focus? If so, what is the cost of that? When you are performing at your peak — perhaps in the zone or flow state — what is your focus on and what is your state of stress and performance at those times? Furthermore, are the motivators intrinsic and self-chosen or extrinsic and driven by external rewards? For example, you may be very helpful to others but what is the reason for doing that? Is it because it is its own reward and gives you a deep level of satisfaction, or is it because it will look good in the eyes of others and will help you to get ahead? Why do you work hard at your job? Is it because you are passionate about it and feel that it does something useful in the world, or is it because you want a promotion, power or a pay rise? There's nothing wrong with doing well in your job, but the question is about what your primary motivation is. What would we put first, and what would we be prepared to forego?

The leader's way: Awareness

Drawing together the insights, research, focus questions and experiments we've explored above, a foundational leadership attribute for prioritizing well is *awareness*. Just like authenticity is a master key to leading with purpose, so awareness is a master key to prioritizing well as a leader. A bit like a ceiling light in a dark room, the light of awareness helps leaders to see where they need to give their energy and time, and from where they need to withdraw it. With awareness, leaders can step back and gain clarity on what they need to prioritize. With awareness, leaders are more attuned to distractions and disruptions that, if unaddressed, will derail and dilute focus from the most important priorities. Below are some personal practices and policy recommendations that are useful for leaders who want to have their priorities informed by greater awareness. The cost of distraction and cognitive overload matters for all workers, but when these problems affect a leader that then sets the tone and culture for others working within the team or organization. The leader must lead by example.

Personal practices

Practice 1: Be the master by reducing addiction to your technology and managing it wisely

Here are a few simple strategies that can help wean you off an over-dependence on your technology. Firstly, draw some boundaries around it. Particularly avoid it invading your personal life and space, especially in bed at night. Secondly, make a commitment to yourself to have a technology-free time in your day, day in your week and week in your year. It will be hard at first, but you will be thankful if you stick with it. Thirdly, turn off all the notifications and delete all apps you don't really need and use. Fourthly, take care about where you take your technology. For example, do you really need it in the meeting room and, if you do have it with you, then at the very least, get it out of eyesight.

Practice 2: Let the light in: Learn to manage your attention by practising mindfulness regularly

Un-fog your mind. Punctuate your day with at least two full stops (i.e. a meditation practice for five minutes or more) and lots of commas (i.e. a mini-meditation from 15 seconds up to two minutes). Good times for the full stops are before you get to work, and then between your working day and whatever activities you are going to do after work. Commas are particularly useful between the completion of one thing (e.g. working on writing a report) and the commencement of another (e.g. heading off to a meeting). Then live and work mindfully (i.e. practise paying attention in the present moment to one thing, one job, one moment at a time as you move through your working day).

Practice 3: Declutter the room by reducing cognitive load wherever and whenever possible

Conserve energy and mental space by having downtime and especially by keeping simple moments simple. For example, there is no need to complicate a 5-minute walk from the train station to your office, or from the office to a meeting, with 5 minutes of rumination and worry. Give yourself 5 minutes of mental space by just walking and, in the process, cultivate a clear, attentive state of mind to take into the next complex activity. Also, get away from the desk, especially during a meal break. Next, chunk or compartmentalize your time by just working on one thing at a time rather than jumping in a rapid and reactive way between things, such as from reading a report to an email notification to an unplanned conversation to an incoming slack message, etc. until you have about 20 jobs open and half done at the same time. Do one task for as long as you need to (e.g. planning a new initiative), then have a comma, then move on to the next priority (e.g. opening your email), and working on that, then have a comma, and then move to the next task (e.g. going to a meeting), etc. If you do have to break the flow of a task due to an unexpected but important priority, then so be it. Deal with it and then come back to what you were doing before. In this way, practise efficient attention switching, not complex multitasking.

Policy recommendations

» *Recommendation 1: Do not complex multitask.* This was mentioned as a personal priority above, but also make it a workplace policy. Encourage staff to learn efficient attention switching, to compartmentalize time, and to do one task at a time before moving on to the next one. If possible, keep meetings free of technology like smartphones, and only have laptops in the room and open if they are actually being used for the meeting.

» *Recommendation 2: Prioritize time for the important, non-urgent parts of work.* Let — in fact, encourage — staff and yourself to have downtime in order to reduce mental load. This is particularly useful as a mental preparation before taking time to do something creative or to reflect on non-urgent but important, big-picture items of their work priorities. Allow space for standing back from work and looking at what is being done, why it is being done, and how it is being done. Prioritize time in the day and week to sit back and be creative, or to do some blue-sky thinking. You might even mandate a quiet, contemplative workspace for this (non)activity.

» *Recommendation 3: Encourage switching off at a reasonable time rather than being always on.* Collectively discuss and agree on shared policies around when staff are encouraged to switch on and off from work-related activities. Some workplaces take the next step and even turn off their email servers at a particular time in the evening (e.g. 7 p.m.) and only turn them on again at a particular time in the morning (e.g. 7 a.m.). If you and your staff can protect time to refuel and refresh each evening then it will be repaid with interest the next day when a less depleted and more energized employee turns up to work.

Summary

In this chapter, we have explored how cognitive overload and not managing the input of information lead to poorer attentional capacities and a reduced ability to prioritize. There are flow-on effects to motivation, decision-making, performance and mental health. Cultivating greater awareness through a more mindful way of working helps enormously to increase focus but also to cultivate the self-awareness and metacognition required to prioritize better and with more discernment. To that end, a range of experiments and practices have been provided that you and your staff can use right away. Importantly, in order to see their potential, make a commitment to consistently apply these practices over a series of weeks and not just for a day or two.

Chapter 4

People

On 15 March 2019, a horrendous gun massacre took place in two mosques in Christchurch, New Zealand, leaving 50 innocent worshippers dead. Jacinda Ardern, New Zealand's then prime minister, responded not only swiftly, but with compassion, respect and authenticity. Her words of consolation and photos of her comforting the bereaved were beamed far and wide. Not surprisingly, she was lauded around the world for her leadership and capacity to unify the community at a time when there was significant risk of splintering and conflict.[1] What grabbed the world's attention wasn't so much related to policy, management or law enforcement — although there were many decisions relating to that too — but rather her ability to relate from the heart to the whole community, Muslim and non-Muslim alike, at a time when so many were shocked and grieving after this brutal act.

Ardern's leadership over this incident earned her credibility and political capital which lasted years afterwards. It was a natural consequence of her humane and compassionate response.

Jacinda Ardern is far from the only example of the human qualities which people most value and respect in leaders. Martin Luther King Jr was the leading figure and inspiration behind the civil rights movement in the United States. His 'I Have a Dream' speech at the Lincoln Memorial is one of the most moving ever made and summed up his ethos of common humanity which transcended race.[2] Mother Teresa was a humble nun but she inspired a worldwide movement dedicated to charity and selfless service for which she won the Nobel Peace Prize in 1997.[3] Winston Churchill, through his wartime speeches, is credited with inspiring England's indomitable resistance to the might of Nazi Germany in World War II. As he said at the time, 'It was the nation … that had the lion's heart. I had the luck to be called upon to give the roar.'[4] Angela Merkel was one of the longest-serving German chancellors and an admired leader around the world. Her nickname was 'Mutti Merkel' which translates as 'Mother Merkel' because of the compassion and care she was known for.

None of these leaders is without human flaws and it is not our intention to suggest any of them were perfect, did not have their critics and never made a poor decision. The point is that these and many other potential examples demonstrate that leadership is about much more than just making astute policy decisions, as important as that is. At the core of leadership is connecting with people: understanding what inspires and moves them, knowing what is in their hearts and being able to give voice to that. If leadership was merely about driving a machine like a car, then it would be relatively easy and predictable, but people are not machines. The ability to lead effectively depends on the ability of the leader to relate to people, whether it is an electorate or a work team, and to be able to communicate effectively. The intellect may well set the direction, but the emotions provide the impetus and energy to move in that direction. To do this, the leader must be in touch with the emotional state and potential of their followers but also understand the barriers, such as their fears or concerns, which may affect them. It is hard to make progress without recognizing, acknowledging and removing those barriers.

A gifted leader can tap a deep well of emotional reserves within themselves and in so doing draw that out of others, whether the emotion needed in a situation is compassion, a sense of fairness, courage or steely resolve. But emotional insight and drive is not enough by itself. An equally gifted but less well-motivated leader also understands people's emotional states and can inspire them but also deceive them at the same time, leading to some horrendous outcomes. Therefore, there is also a need for intellect and ethical principles to guide and regulate the emotional energy.

Leaders and managers

It has long been said that there are two kinds of people in positions of authority: leaders and managers. They might seem like they are different words for the same thing, but they are very different functions. An article in the *Harvard Business Review* put it this way. Managers focus on 'building competence, control, and the appropriate balance of power' but this doesn't take into account 'the essential leadership elements of inspiration, vision and human passion — which drive corporate success.'[5] A true leader is a leader of people and not just a manager of projects. Clearly, an excellent leader can also have excellent managerial skills, but they don't necessarily arise in the same person. In such a case, the visionary and inspiring leader certainly needs good managers around them to be sure that the vision is delivered effectively and that the inspiration, passion and energy are directed where they are most useful.

Given the previous chapters, where some of the pitfalls associated with the misuse and overuse of information technologies have been dealt with at length, one could easily think this book is anti-technology or anti-social media. Not so. Technology and social media can also be powerful tools for transformation when used well. Consider the profoundly inspiring leadership of Ukrainian President Volodymyr Zelenskyy. With (almost) universal admiration, in late 2022 Zelenskyy was chosen as *Time Magazine*'s person of the year for his inspirational leadership of the Ukrainian people following the invasion by Russia. When he was first elected, many people did not take him very seriously as a leader. With his media and comedy acting background many saw him as a lightweight, but that view has been turned 180 degrees with his unwavering and inspiring wartime leadership. He has inspired the much smaller country of Ukraine to defiantly take on the much larger military might of Russia. Ukraine has not only punched well above its weight militarily, but through Zelenskyy's impassioned political advocacy and his ability to connect with people through conventional and social media, he and Ukraine have won the hearts and minds of people all around the world. Clearly, he has disciplined and very intelligent strategists around him, but if Ukraine is the lion of the 2020s, then undoubtedly Zelenskyy has given it its roar. He has accurately read and given expression to the mood of his people and proved to be a gifted leader in every sense of the word.

There are many other modern examples of inspiring and visionary leaders, such as Malala Yousafzai, the Pakistani education activist; Nelson Mandela, the South African anti-apartheid campaigner; and Aung San Suu Kyi, the Burmese politician and diplomat. But the same qualities that these people show on the global stage (e.g. inspiration, courage, perseverance, a desire for justice) is just as well illustrated on a small scale by many of the leaders we meet in everyday life. Consider the qualities of the most inspiring leaders you have experienced in your own life, whether at school, work or at your local sporting club. It is not their managerial skills that draw people like magnets. Equally, inspired leadership without sound management will soon lose its way and founder.

If leaders can be inspirational, so too can they crush inspiration and innovation, especially when they view their leadership role as primarily managerial and lose sight of the fact that they are leading people, not programming machines. One unit within a large organization gives an illustrative example. It was originally noted for its innovation, energy, can-do culture and very high output. It was a leader in its field largely due to the vision of its founding leader, who built the unit on a culture of choosing new employees based on their energy, character and innovative spirit. They were expected to contribute to a variety of established projects, but they were also encouraged to be creative and use their talents to break new ground and develop their areas of passion. This was seen as a key part of their role. The unit's leader encouraged new employees to have a go and, if it worked out well, build on the success, but if it wasn't successful then learn from the experience, move on and try again. This unit was also noted as being an energetic and happy place to work and that environment continued for many years with subsequent leaders having been brought up in that same culture.

Eventually, a new leader was needed but the selection process was largely undertaken by people within the wider organization who were not particularly familiar with the culture in that unit. The new person, Diane, was chosen but her style was more managerial than leadership oriented. She was ambitious and primarily valued strategic plans and performance metrics more than people. Diane was successful in her own field but that sphere of interest was largely the focus of her attention. Wanting to be successful and to climb the institutional ladder, she didn't value helping others to shine if their talents and passions didn't align with hers. Hence, new employees were chosen specifically to further her sphere of interest.

Established and respected employees who had developed their spheres of expertise merely became cogs in a machine to further Diane's priorities. There was little encouragement — in fact, there was discouragement — for people to develop capabilities outside of her narrow sphere of interest. Diane's people skills were not her strong suit, and when even quite senior members of that unit were told what they were now expected to focus on, there was no inspiration or big picture presented, just 'I need you to do this'. If that employee made the case for building on the expertise they had established over many years, it was suggested that they would need to shift their focus to the new agenda or they would do well to leave and work somewhere else. Needless to say, it was a far less happy place to work. A lot of very talented and devoted people left that unit in the following few years and it is no longer noted for innovation.

One way of understanding the above example is the famous distinction between 'transactional' and 'transformational' forms of leadership, first coined by James McGregor Burns in the 1970s and developed by Bernard Bass in the 1980s. *Transactional* leadership is where the leader sets clear goals and objectives for their team and intervenes when these are not met. As the name suggests, it involves a transactional mindset, where staff members work on tasks in exchange for goal-clarity, performance accountability and financial reward. Diane's leadership in the above case has some of the (less healthy) hallmarks of transactional leadership.

By contrast, *transformational* leaders focus on inspiring followers to achieve ambitious and meaningful goals, providing a high level of intellectual stimulation, and connecting personally and authentically with followers (known as 'individualized consideration'). Although both styles have their place, studies have shown that, compared with transactional leadership, transformational leadership consistently leads to greater employee performance, motivation and commitment.[7] These impacts have been shown across different industries, managerial environments and national cultures. We are not suggesting that setting clear goals and holding staff accountable is not important. On the contrary, these are critical skills for any leader. Transactional leadership, however, is not enough for building a strong and healthy culture, as the above example highlights.

Focus Question 1: What were the human qualities you most respected in the best leaders you have had? It is worthwhile taking some time to reflect on the human qualities you most admired in leaders you know or have worked under. Was it their ability to listen, question or show respect even to those they disagreed with? Was it their directness, authenticity or coolness under fire? It could be many other things. Ask yourself, how were those qualities conveyed or manifested? Was it in their words, tone of voice, behaviour or decisions? What was the effect on you and others they were leading? Could these leadership qualities really be conveyed adequately through a tweet, via an email or similar media compared to being conveyed in-person?

Emotional intelligence, stress and burnout

Eleanor Roosevelt once said: 'A good leader inspires people to have confidence in the leader, a great leader inspires people to have confidence in themselves.' Leadership is all about people. Great leaders don't just lead the minds of those who follow them, they inspire them. For that to happen a leader needs to be very aware and emotionally in touch with the people they are leading. They also need to be able to communicate with clarity, precision and simplicity, but also with heart. It requires presence, as well as social and emotional intelligence.

That seems simple enough but it is not so easy. A variety of factors can undermine these qualities and abilities in a leader. An always-on culture causes two main problems with leading people in this way. One is that when a leader starts to feel stretched, overloaded and mentally fatigued, their capacity to engage authentically with others rapidly deteriorates. The science of this is relatively simple. When a person's stress circuits in the brain (the amygdala) are firing off because they perceive a major threat (or an accumulation of small threats) then they mobilize the one-dimensional fight or flight response. This response is great for reacting instinctively or quickly — like climbing a tree to get away from a tiger — but it is not so good for the multidimensional and nuanced capabilities required to communicate effectively and clearly with people. The executive functioning circuits in the prefrontal cortex (the leadership level of the brain) are 'hijacked' by the stress circuits, meaning we replace considered and attentive responses with automatic pilot reactions. In this mode, we switch to a 'default response', which is a kind of mental shortcut and less energy intensive. This, for most of us, is a transactional approach to leading — just getting the basics done and surviving — rather than transformational leadership, which tends to be more of an effort for people who are not used to this way of working and leading.

The second factor is that a sustained cognitive load and 'info-whelm' predisposes a person to mental fatigue and eventually burnout. There are three main hallmarks of burnout as originally described by Christina Maslach and Susan Jackson: emotional exhaustion (feeling emotionally wrung out by work), decreased personal accomplishment (not feeling like anything useful is being achieved), and depersonalization (a sense of disconnection and indifference to the needs of others).[8] Hallmarks of burnout have since been extended to include lack of professional efficacy and cynicism. From a people leadership perspective, depersonalization is perhaps the key burnout factor. Depersonalization means that the person stops caring in the same way by taking up a distant or indifferent attitude towards the people they work with and for. It can also manifest as negative, callous and cynical behaviours and impersonal interactions, which is particularly problematic for those in caring roles or trying to support others.[9]

Furthermore, withdrawal is a commonly used coping mechanism and, although it is understandable, it is not a particularly adaptive one. When our own cognitive and emotional resources are depleted, we naturally do what we can to conserve them, just like people hoard food and water if they fear a famine or drought coming. Disengaging from more direct, authentic and open conversations with those we lead is a very basic response to feeling overwhelmed. This is a wake-up for the leader themselves, which should alert them to how they are looking after themselves (or not). It can, and often does, have a massive impact on interpersonal connection with team members and sets a tone for the workplace, which others may soon follow. This is one of the major reasons why we say, often, self-care is not selfish or self-indulgent; it is a responsibility of an effective leader.

If you are leading others then chances are you will be giving a lot of yourself, but are you also taking time to renew yourself? This could include lifestyle measures such as taking time for physical exercise. We will explore this in far more detail in Chapter 5, but in brief, if we don't take time to renew ourselves, our well will soon run dry. Then it is hard for anyone to draw from it.

Technology and text don't replace conversation

Even when a leader has capacity and energy, tech-mediated work environments lend themselves to text-based communication as the default (e.g. collaboration apps, email and texting). In most workplaces, these ways of communicating are replacing more authentic, face-to-face conversations. Tech-mediated communication is time-efficient and good for getting some things done, but it lacks most of the empathy, nuance and body language that is a part of deeper communication and necessary for supporting social and emotional intelligence.

With text-based communications via text messages or email it is so much easier to project one's own attitude or mood onto what the other person has written. If, for example, we are angry over something that has just happened, then we easily read anger into what someone has written. If we are feeling irritated then it is easier to read tongue-in-cheek humour as a jibe or cynicism. Research shows that even when people are communicating with a cool head, they are able to accurately identify the other person's emotion only 50 per cent of the time when sending a text-based message.[10] In this study, 15 per cent of the time the person entirely mistook the positive or negative valence of the other's emotion (i.e. the extent to which an emotion is positive or negative). In a pressured work environment, the results are likely to be far worse.

To illustrate, an executive who was participating in a mindfulness course gave an example of being time poor and quickly reading a customer's email. He immediately jumped to the conclusion that the customer was being difficult and obstructive and he was about to smash out an abrasive reply. Luckily, the executive had a moment of awareness where he noticed himself acting on automatic pilot and that there was a distinct possibility he was making assumptions about the customer's purpose in writing the email. He paused, then decided he needed to send a more measured response asking for clarification about what the customer actually needed. The customer responded that he was just asking for some further information to help make his decision. The executive sent an amicable response providing the further information and all was well.

Such problems are compounded when, as a leader, you need to dig a bit deeper and check in on how team member is tracking, and what is going on for them. It's even worse when things aren't working and there is disengagement or even inter-personal conflict. What we see in such situations is that leaders often struggle to realize what the need is and then switch gears and pick up a different communication approach. This sounds very basic, and it is, but it is incredible how often we see this done poorly. This misreading of others is far less likely to happen if we are communicating more directly, face-to-face with a person and we have other cues like the tone of their voice and their body language to help us to calibrate or correct our perceptions. Our work with leaders in cultivating mindful ways of leading provides valuable insights into this. Studies have found that people who are more mindful seem to communicate differently to those who are less so. Comparing professionals with highest and lowest mindfulness scores, more mindful professionals are more client-centred, engage in more rapport building, display more positive emotional tone and are more likely to rate highly on communication and have satisfied clients.[11]

Practical experiment 1: Check your perceptions

Notice an occasion when you read a text-based communication that produces an emotive effect on you. Observe the effect and your reaction. What kind of text-based response would you feel tempted to write? Then, if possible, take the opportunity to see the person face to face or phone them to have a conversation about it. Begin by inviting them to give you the message verbally. If it's not clear, check with them that you understand the key elements of their message's content and tone. What was the effect of the verbal message and your reaction? Was your perception of it the same as the text-based message? Was your verbal response the same as the text-based one you were tempted to write?

Communicating and working in teams

A research project we were peripherally involved with was instigated via an email exchange between two people who knew of each other but didn't know each other. Other potential collaborators were emailed to invite their involvement and they joined in too. Most of the people, however, had never met and the planning for this research project all took place via text-based communication. As the project unfolded, planning seemed to be a laborious process. Simple questions took a string of emails to resolve with any level of agreement. As more questions arose, engagement became lower and people responded to emails in a less timely manner. In the end, the project got done but it was not particularly successful or enjoyable and there was no desire among team members to collaborate again as a group. One wonders what difference a few face-to-face conversations might have made.

A US study looked at how teams approached complex problems. It found that when people use text-based communication (rather than a more direct, conversational approach) to collaborate on a complex work problem, it undermined the quality of their engagement and interpersonal connection for subsequent tasks.[12] In other words, there is a spill-over effect that means people are less motivated and feel less connected in tackling whatever the next task or challenge is.

For these reasons, we see that an always-on culture and the overuse of text-based collaboration can quickly drain teams and their leaders of their 'social capital', unless this is addressed consciously. People need to be able to have spaces for direct communication in which they can share their personal challenges, be heard and feel supported. Similarly, team members need to receive direct feedback, and be able to feel clear about what they need to do to grow and improve. These conversations cannot happen in a rush or via an email and, in some places, they simply do not happen at all. Switching gears from a fast-paced 'plan, do and move-on' approach to building deeper connections within teams is the point of difference here. However, it is hard, if not impossible, for stretched, time-poor leaders to do that unless an effort is made to reduce the cognitive load and the deluge of information and messages that is causing it.

Another area of interesting research explores the impact of an always-on way of working on people's ability to regulate their emotions in social interactions. For many teams and their leaders, device-use seems to be interrupting the quality of human connection. The smartphone is perhaps the clearest example of this. This revolution in connectivity has made communication quicker and more flexible than ever before. But it has brought with it a dependence that undermines people's capacity to communicate more directly, face to face. As a result, research on tech addiction has exploded in recent years.

Studies have shown that the chronic and compulsive use of devices impacts people's social cognition, which includes key psychological 'resources' such as self-esteem and self-concept.[13,14] Social cognition can be defined as the 'psychological processes that enable individuals to take advantage of being part of a social group'."[15] With strong social cognition, people have the capacity to build connections and mutual trust with others, to accurately read others' intentions and interpret their behaviours and receive support when needed. Research that we have conducted has found that the compulsive use of devices consistently erodes elements of social cognition, such as self-esteem and hope, and leads to difficulties in regulating emotions, including less emotional intelligence and difficulties pursuing goals in the presence of negative emotions.[16] These are critical skills for leaders, who need to be able to regulate their own emotional reactions to situations to maintain team focus and stay on track.

It's not just team members or followers who suffer from working with leaders who are overly tied to their devices. It seems to work the other way as well. Research, including a study we have undertaken, found that compulsive online use leads to reduced reach to social support, including less connection with others and less capacity to access tangible help and support.[17,18] Rather than acting as a substitute for high-quality connection, it appears that compulsive tech-use undermines the quality of social support people receive, which is critical for leaders. As the old saying goes, 'it's lonely at the top'. Rather than strengthening leaders' connection with their team members and other key collaborators, when virtual interactions displace face to face or at least real-time connection (e.g. Zoom), the quality of connection suffers. This, of course, has downstream impacts not just on the leader themselves, but also on those they lead. Feeling less supported and connected, the quality of trust breaks down, or is just never really established. As we know, trust is essential for a safe and enjoyable workplace and is a foundation stone of building a high-performing team and organization.

Focus Question 2: Have you ever found yourself using text and technology as a way of avoiding direct contact with colleagues? Why? If you have found yourself increasingly having virtual communications with colleagues at the expense of more direct conversations, have you observed a tendency to retreat to that, particularly as a way of avoiding challenging conversations about important issues? If so, did that help to resolve the issue or compound it in the longer run? When avoiding something, is your mind at rest or is it agitated and preoccupied about the thing that is being avoided? When you eventually confront the issue you were avoiding, what is the effect on your state of mind?

Dialectic: The art of inquiry

Since the time of the ancient Greeks, the art of asking questions has been central to the pursuit of knowledge in all its forms, particularly wisdom. This art, in its purest form, is called dialectic. Often, we are so ready and willing to communicate to others what we want to say that we forget to inquire into what others have to say. We are so ready and willing to prove ourselves right and others wrong that we don't rationally question our own or anybody else's assumptions.

The whole process of a dialectic approach is based on 'education' in the true sense of the word. Education comes from a Latin word, *educare*, meaning 'to lead or draw out'. Real education is not a process of stuffing knowledge in, as is the common view, but a process of drawing out the wisdom or insight that is latent within us. What is that inherent wisdom covered by? False opinions. What removes those false opinions? Sincere, honest and courageous questioning.

Dialectic, at its best, is an ego-free exploration of an issue. You might have already noticed that when the ego gets involved in a conversation it quickly makes things personal. The conversation becomes about winning or losing an argument, not an inquiry into the truth or strength of a position. This readily leads to feeling threatened if we are proved wrong, in which case we will fight to win any way we can. That means conflict, distorting or misrepresenting the other's view, hiding inconvenient aspects of our own view, and ignoring any evidence that makes our position weaker. We may win the argument, but merit or the truth is then sacrificed at the altar of our ego, and our relationship with those involved may go the same way. Even if we are correct about something, when the ego gets involved, the focus becomes power or self-aggrandisement rather than truth, and this potentially demeans or humiliates the other. Egoless exploration of an issue is always a collaborative rather than a competitive process.

Focus Question 3: Can we create greater self-awareness when discussing important issues? See if you can become more aware of yourself in the process of exploring issues and having debates. Have you noticed the effect of being attached to your points of view or positions? What is the effect on how you feel and how you communicate? Does it make the conversation personal? Does it create the potential for threat if we are at risk of being proved wrong about something? What is the effect of noticing that and letting go of the need to be right? Can we objectively and impartially question ours and others' assumptions? What is the effect of that on how you feel and how you communicate?

Practical experiment 2: Dialectic inquiry

Dialectic works better if we follow a few basic principles. First, in our attitude, seek the truth rather than being right or winning. This changes the conversation into a collaborative process rather than one of conflict. Second, to prioritize the truth of an issue or business problem we will need to let go of our attachment to our opinions. See them more as ideas being examined or put under scrutiny. Third, with a free mind, collaboratively question the opinion, position or view being put forward. Test it and see if it stands up to scrutiny and evidence. Fourth, if it doesn't then discard it and, based on insights gleaned, consider again. Fifth, in the process of discussion, really listen to others, as well as yourself. For leaders of teams and businesses, this dialectic approach always makes for better decisions. Rather than pushing a pet opinion or project, the dialectic leader who is focused on the truth of an issue or problem will inevitably end up making contributions that are more accurate, less biased, and more focused on addressing the actual crux of whatever issue or challenge is on the table.

Empathy and compassion are not the same thing

Being a people-focused leader sounds like an excellent idea and seems simple, but people and human interactions are complex, largely because of the emotions that are a natural part of being human. Empathy is one such emotion. For decades now we have been told about the importance of empathy and how to cultivate it but there is a rethink underway about whether that has been entirely good advice. The emerging scientific consensus is that empathy is useful to a point but it's what happens next, *after* we experience empathy, that makes all the difference as to whether it is a positive or negative thing.

New research from the domains of psychology, physiology and neurology on the nature of empathy and compassion has completely revolutionized our thinking. The key points are indicated in the following figure on the hierarchy model of empathy and compassion by Singer and Klimecki.[19]

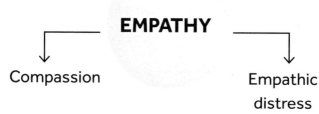

EMPATHY

Compassion

Empathic distress

Other-related emotion
Positive feelings:
e.g., love
Good health
Approach & prosocial
motivation

Self-related emotion
Negative feelings: e.g.,
stress
Poor health, burnout
Withdrawal & non-social
behavior

Figure 1.

When we experience empathy for another — perhaps a work colleague is in distress because of a troublesome relationship with a team member — then we arrive at an important fork in the road. Empathy most commonly takes the next step into 'empathic distress', meaning we are distressed by the colleague's distress. It's also called 'vicarious distress'. Our brain and body's stress pathways fire off in the same way as those of the person experiencing the original distress. That can, and generally does, quickly cascade to negative emotions, focusing attention on ourselves and a desire to put ourselves out of distress by quickly 'fixing' the other. If we are consistently confronted by such empathic distress and activating these stress pathways, then our health can suffer, we experience empathy fatigue and eventually burnout. One commonly used way to protect ourselves is to withdraw.[20] This is a lose–lose situation. If empathy takes this path, then it is not so useful.

Focus Question 4: What is the effect of empathic distress? Without judgment or criticism, take this opportunity to reflect on a time when you experienced empathic or vicarious distress. Perhaps it was a time when someone close to you was suffering in some way, or when someone you are responsible for was not performing or coping well. Were you in control of your emotions or were they in control of you? What was the effect on your physical state? Did you notice signs of activating the fight or flight response like tension, adrenaline, racing heart, breathing fast and activation? What was the effect on your emotional state? Did you feel afraid, rushed, agitated, confused, frozen or angry? What was the effect on your behaviour? Did you want to fight or fly (escape) or feel anxious to quickly fix the situation? What was the effect on your communication? Were you distracted, flustered, verbose or shut down? What was the effect on how you felt afterwards and were those residual effects obvious for minutes, hours or days? What was the effect on your openness to being confronted by a similar situation in the future?

An unhealthy way of protecting ourselves from the distress is to assume that we need to become unfeeling to the distress of others as the only option. Not so. If, on the other hand, the empathy moves into 'compassion' then the concern and attention is focused on the other person rather than being turned back on ourselves. This leads to activation of circuits in the brain associated with positive emotions, which results in better mental and physical health as well as prosocial behaviour directed at helping the other if possible.

Sometimes there is no action required but we simply need to create a safe space for the person to speak about what is going on for them. Either way, stepping into compassion is a win–win situation — the helper and the one needing the help are both better for it. On the basis of increasing research, experts are arguing that in reality there is no such thing as compassion fatigue. People do not experience compassion and distress at the same time. Compassion does not fatigue people, it energizes them.

Qualitative evidence shows that training in mindfulness and compassion for leaders impacts on two axes: self versus others, and attitudes versus behaviours.[21]As far as self is concerned, such training leads to attitude change (greater self-awareness, open-mindedness and insight) as well as behaviour changes (better emotional self-regulation, letting go of unhelpful behaviours and developing helpful ones). As far as others are concerned, the training leads to attitude changes (greater awareness of impact on others, open-mindedness to others, making allowances for others' difficult emotions and greater appreciation of others) and behaviour changes (effective communication, better directions, empowering others and greater care).

'Just turn empathy into compassion' sounds easy but it does require that we practise a few things. The question is whether we can notice these signs a little sooner, like when they are actually happening and, if so, can we do something different amid the reaction and turn it more into a conscious and useful response? If you have been practising some of the previously described mindfulness skills then this will make the whole process a lot easier.

Practical experiment 3: Practise turning empathy into compassion

Here are four key steps that can help you turn empathy into compassion. First, we need awareness, including self-awareness, to notice ourselves in the moment of reacting to another's distress. This is a prerequisite for the next step — being able to consciously choose our response. Second, we need to teach ourselves to be accepting and comfortable with discomfort that we and the other person might be experiencing. If we can't do that, then our attention will turn away from the situation and we may well react too quickly in terms of hastily trying to 'fix' it. Third, we need to remember our common humanity in that this person wishes to be free of suffering, just like ourselves. This is important for garnering our resources to help the person in front of us if indeed it is possible to provide help. Fourth, if we have navigated our way through the first three steps, we need to impartially but compassionately engage our attention on the other person and their situation, listen carefully and be open to helping if help is possible. Now we have transformed empathy into compassion. No matter how well or poorly you feel you handled the situation, learn from your experience and move on. And as with all these leadership skills, be prepared to practise this a number of times before a compassionate response starts to become more natural and spontaneous.

The aware leader as a role-model

For better or worse, a leader is a powerful role-model for their organization or team. Team members are far more likely to do what a leader does rather than what they say, at least, while the leader isn't watching. Therefore, acting more consciously is central to the leader being able to set the example they wish others to follow. This can be illustrated by reference to the emerging evidence in the field.

The disposition of a leader to be more aware (trait mindfulness) predicts a range of outcomes on employee wellbeing and performance.[22] A mindful leader, just by virtue of the fact that they are more present and attentive to those they are working with, positively impacts job satisfaction and psychological need satisfaction (i.e. autonomy, competence and relatedness) as well as positively affecting job performance and organizational citizenship behaviours (i.e. actions or initiatives that go beyond your direct role, but that benefit others in your team or the wider organization). Psychological need satisfaction plays an important role in explaining why leaders' mindfulness strengthens employees' performance — the more the leader is attentive to and supports the psychological needs of their staff the better they perform and the more fulfilled they are.[23] Mindfulness also predicts ethical and prosocial behaviours because people who are more aware are more intrinsically motivated and make more conscious rather than habitual choices.[24]

Research on the effect of mindfulness on senior managers finds that it enhances participants' leadership skills. In particular, it inspires a shared vision, demonstrates moral intelligence, and encourages and motivates others.[25] A more mindful leader positively impacts various aspects of followers' satisfaction,[26] mainly due to the leader's communication with their followers. The role of mindfulness in improving the ability to manage emotional ups and downs in the workplace may be of central importance in large part because it buffers against the negative effect of rumination and negative emotions that turn negative experiences (e.g. experiencing an injustice) into negative behaviours (e.g. retaliation).[27, 28] When a negative behaviour leads to retaliation then it more deeply ingrains resentment, animosity and further poor behaviour. The capacity to be present and self-aware may be central to curbing workplace aggression. Awareness plays a critical role in preventing hostility from turning into aggression.[29] Awareness is particularly helpful because of its capacity to reduce the extent to which individuals feel compelled to unconsciously and habitually use the unhelpful emotion regulation approaches that often escalate conflict, like suppression, acting out and negative communication. Leader mindfulness also helps people to manage their emotional exhaustion, so it does not spiral into poor mood and abusive supervision.[30]

Evidence on the relationship between mindfulness and perceptions of team-member exchange (TMX, i.e. a workers' perception of the quality of working relationships as a whole within the team) indicates that mindfulness is significantly and positively related to TMX mainly due to its role in enhancing the ability to manage emotions.[31] As such it may be a vital tool for team building and reducing workplace conflict.[32] 'Team mindfulness' is therefore an emerging concept.[33] Such abilities work as a safeguard against escalating team conflict and reduce the tendency for task conflict to turn into relationship conflict and, as a result, undermining among other team members.

Helping employees to be more aware helps them as well. Leader awareness is beneficially associated with employee wellbeing as measured by reduced emotional exhaustion, increased job satisfaction and satisfying psychological needs, and with better job performance. The study also stressed the important role that the organizational environment plays in promoting or hindering employee mindfulness at the workplace.[34]

The leader's way: Openness

Once again, we are left with the need to articulate an enduring leadership trait that goes to the heart of the potential problems that leaders face in connecting better with the people they work with, and not one that merely numbs us or distracts us. Drawing together the stories and research we outline above, we see an attitude of *openness* as perhaps the most valuable underlying attribute leaders can cultivate in building strong, healthy connections with those they lead. Openness is about your heart, your attitude. It's about the way you enter situations, meetings, debates, conflicts and conversations. With a fundamental attitude of openness, your 'baggage' is left at the door, and you show up fully for the situation you find yourself in. Only when we're open are we able to connect clearly and fully with the individual or individuals in our sphere, or the system we are working in. Only when we're open are we truly able to meet someone — particularly if it's someone we've worked or lived with for decades. When we are open, it's as if we're meeting the person or situation for the very first time. We are meeting them freshly, ready for whatever the meeting or situation turns up. This, then, opens the door to authenticity; transformational leadership; regulating, but also not hiding, emotions; showing compassion; and all the elements we've unpacked above.

In cultivating openness, the leader doesn't need to become a doormat for all sorts of agendas, become un-strategic, or say 'yes' to everything. It is absolutely possible as a leader to engage openly with others, while at the same time being savvy and, when needed, digging in and standing your ground. Being open is about being fully present and fully engaged — even if it's in a situation of conflict, or where intense debate or immense persistence is needed. By being open, we're more attuned to the various cues in our environment — which means we're not just connecting authentically with others; we are also taking in a fuller picture of the attitudes, information and preferences that others are providing, what is at stake and how to best respond. Being open, we are better able to actually *hear* what people are saying, including the agendas, ambitions and aspirations that shape them. Below, we offer three personal practices that cultivate leadership openness.

Practical experiment 1: Communicate with openness and attention

First, by all means, do your homework before having an important conversation or meeting, but take care not to have the conversation in your head a number of times before you have it with the person. Such a habit puts words into the other's mouth and projects attitudes onto them that generally have nothing to do with reality. We might think that we are practising or rehearsing, but it is generally rumination pretending to be useful. Avoiding this will reduce the risk of you prejudicing the conversation if/when the time comes and closing down your range of responses. Second, pause, be present and centre yourself prior to, and on the way to, the conversation. Third, when the time comes, pause at the commencement of the conversation, then communicate with attention, particularly in relation to the listening side of the equation. Notice how often the listening disengages from what the other person is saying and turns inward to you habitually mentally rehearsing what you are about to say in response. This is an example of the 'baggage' we mentioned above. Turn your attention outwards and keep listening. Be sure that you understand the other before seeking to make yourself understood. Ask questions where needed to be sure that you have a clear picture of what is going on for the other. Then, in responding, speak with openness. Acknowledge and address what the other person or people have raised alongside anything you need to say.

Practical experiment 2: Learn to mindfully regulate emotions

We're all human and being more mindful doesn't mean that we will suddenly cease to have uncomfortable emotions, unhelpful reactions and unconscious habits, but we can cultivate our ability to be more aware of them and learn to manage them differently. If you practise mindfulness meditation regularly you are likely to observe a steady flow of emotions, reactions and habits pent up from the day. They will come and go by themselves within the field of your awareness if you let them. We do that by being less reactive to them and cultivating detachment from them. You are not doing something wrong if they arise, but if they do, welcome them and see it as an opportunity to practise letting them come and go with less and less attitude and secondary reactions. This will then give you the wherewithal to notice these emotions, reactions and habits when they arise in the course of your daily interactions with others. Practise watching them with curiosity and cultivating a non-judgmental attitude towards them. You don't have to 'control' these emotions, reactions and habits, but if you learn to stand back from them with non-attachment and a more accepting attitude then you may find that you don't have to be so controlled *by* them. You can watch them without having your attention fixated on and monopolised by them. This will free up your attention to engage with who or what is in front of you and it will also give you a much broader and discerning range of options in response. Importantly, it will help you not to get caught in a cycle of conflict and retaliation when emotional reactions and tensions arise.

Practical experiment 3: Take care with artificial, technological modes of communication

Resist overusing technology. Use it when necessary but, where possible, avoid it replacing real communication with real people. Although there are times when you may need to set boundaries, avoid getting into the habit of side-stepping difficult conversations through virtual modes of communication. Use in-person communication as the first option, and where that is not possible, use verbal forms of communication in preference to sending text messages, particularly in relation to complex, emotive or interpersonal topics. Also, take care not to use technology in such a way that it interferes with engaging with others by complex multitasking while communicating.

Three policy recommendations

» *Recommendation 1: Foster mindful communication.* Whether it is one-on-one interactions or in meetings, foster mindful communication within your team or work culture. Where possible, have someone skilled in this area to come into the workplace to teach these skills to the team.

» *Recommendation 2: Help colleagues develop better emotional regulation.* Help others to understand and cultivate what you have cultivated for yourself. The first step is modelling the behaviour. See this as a part of the culture of how the team or workplace works together. Be patient because this ability takes time to develop.

» *Recommendation 3: Set policies regarding the rational and appropriate use of communication technologies.* Set the Practical experiment 3 as a workplace policy and, in as much as you are able, be a role model for better communication. Do not allow technology to be a division between people while communicating in the workplace or meeting room.

Summary

In this chapter we have explored the importance and complexities of the human aspects of leadership. Many of these are made even more complex by stress, cognitive overload, empathic distress, and the misuse and overuse of technology. Crucial in remedying these problems are the cultivation of an attitude of openness, and associated abilities of self-awareness, dialectic inquiry, compassion and emotional regulation. With a foundational practice of leading with openness, we are able to lead others from a point of being grounded, engaged and, above all, clear.

Chapter 5

Personal

When we're really under pressure trying to juggle too many balls at once, self-care can be the hardest thing to prioritize and the first to go. This is especially the case for leaders. Anyone who has made the jump from being a team member to a manager will know this. You suddenly feel a sense of responsibility that is both exciting and full of potential, but also extremely daunting. Walking this tightrope is a huge challenge for the modern leader — especially in an environment of information overload.

We recently worked with a leader in this situation. Guy was a newly appointed head of his product department at a research and development organization, responsible for around 60 people. We met with Guy several times over his first year in the job, providing coaching support to get him up to speed in his leadership role. We unpacked all sorts of issues and challenges he faced, such as how he shapes and sequences his business priorities, how he deploys his best people, how he handles some tricky individuals, and how he influences the agenda at the top of the organization. But we quickly noticed that Guy was basically running on adrenaline. He wasn't sleeping well. He was responding to emails and other messages at all hours of the night. He was working both days on weekends. Feeling like he had to keep all wheels spinning, he was making very reactive decisions with limited strategy behind them. His energy and attention were all 'out there'. And above all, we saw that he did not have the confidence, or feel he was 'allowed', to pull back and press pause. The net effect was his health was quickly heading south.

Of course, Guy knew this was all happening. He knew he needed to reset the way he was working but couldn't find a circuit-breaker. We worked with him to pull back and get clear on his most important priorities and, critically, identify the balls he was going to consciously drop, and how he would manage that politically so he didn't lose his job. Guy then turned his attention to the way he was working. He identified some boundaries that he was prepared to set around how he used his time so he could get more effective downtime. The biggest challenge in making these changes, Guy said, was guilt. He felt that by putting in place boundaries around his availability, and sticking to them, he was neglecting his team. And yet without those boundaries, he would have lasted another three to six months at best. His self-care and boundary setting were an act of leadership.

Be the change

'Be the change you wish to see in the world.'

There are few more widely cited quotations in the field of leadership than this one commonly attributed to one of the most revered leaders in the 20th century, Mahatma Gandhi, although he may never have actually said it. This quote can be looked at from many different perspectives and from the largest to the smallest scales. One way of considering it is that we can't wish for other people or situations to be different and better than how they are without first personally transforming ourselves, as well as making what we say and do consistent with our noble aspirations. If we can change ourselves for the better then we can at least be at peace with ourselves but we also become a positive influence on the people and situations around us. This was Guy's challenge. As soon as he started setting some boundaries to ensure self-care, it gave permission for others around him to do the same. Arleen Lorrance, an educator at a high school in Brooklyn, New York, put it this way.

> *For seven years I served my sentence and marked off institutional time; I complained, cried, accepted hopelessness, put down the rest of the faculty for all the things they didn't do, and devoted all my energies to trying to change others and the system. It came in on me loud and clear that I was the only one who could imprison (or release) me, that I was the only one I could do anything about changing. So I let go of my anger and*

> negativism and made a decision to simply be totally loving, open and vulnerable all the time.[1]

Being individual parts of a collective, the positive changes we make in ourselves serve as a role model for others. If we change for the better then we are already bringing about cultural change within the organization. Complaining or criticising, on the other hand, can become a part of a workplace culture but, like a black hole, whatever gets sucked into it never returns and it emits no light. Just railing against how things are and wishing that others would be different is not only frustrating and unproductive, but it also sets up a culture of criticism and negativity.

In terms of positive change, we need to start with ourselves. This brings us to the fourth of our four Ps — Personal. There are various ways in which we can explore the personal dimension of leadership. The previous examples hint at the ethical and moral aspects but, as with the case of Guy, the aspects that are perhaps more challenging for the modern leader include, first, self-care amid the oftentimes strident demands of working life and, second, coping with the always-on work environment.

Self-care is not selfish

Olivia was a very committed specialist obstetrician and gynaecologist in her early thirties who had taken up a position in a large regional hospital a year before. The hours were demanding, the work emotionally taxing, and the level of staffing was inadequate to meet the needs. This led to Olivia being asked to do more and longer shifts than would normally be rostered. She unfailingly said yes to such requests because she always put her patients and the hospital first and never wanted to let anyone down. There was inadequate cover to allow for any significant annual leave being taken and as she moved into her second year, feeling tired generally, she took less and less time for things like exercise, leisure activities she really enjoyed, or preparing healthy meals. Even when she wasn't at work physically, she was still mentally preoccupied about it. Olivia avoided raising her concerns with the hospital administration nor did she set reasonable and sustainable limits in terms of how many extra shifts she did. Over time, Olivia's mental health began to suffer and, with that, her work performance. She made a couple of moderately significant clinical errors, which brought things to a head and she was unable to work for some time while she was recovering. Clearly, there are systemic issues that need to be addressed in a scenario like this, but there are also personal issues related to someone not recognizing and acknowledging warning signs earlier, nor feeling that they can and should set reasonable boundaries.

How well we are affects how well we perform. Just to illustrate, US research on hospital doctors — healthcare leaders with high responsibility who are meant to be caring for others — found that at a single point in time, 20 per cent qualified as being depressed and 74 per cent qualified as having burnout on diagnostic rating scales. Of even greater concern was that the depressed doctors made more than six times as many medication and prescribing errors as non-depressed doctors doing the same job.[2] The message: if we are in a position of responsibility and others are within our sphere of care, then self-care is vital for us to be able to perform effectively.

As Guy and Olivia's stories illustrate, many people, including leaders, marginalize the importance of self-care for themselves and their organizations as if it was in some way a distraction or counter to the leaders' and workers' primary responsibilities. Enlightened self-care must therefore be distinguished from things it is commonly confused with, like self-indulgence or selfishness. Those are entirely different things. Self-care is about *need*. It is related to doing the things necessary for us to be able to function in a happy, sustainable and effective way. As the research on hospital doctors illustrates, if we are not well, then we can't do our job effectively or safely. Self-indulgence and selfishness, on the other hand, involve doing things that may be pleasurable but are not necessary for our own wellbeing, nor are they aimed at helping us to help others. Self-indulgence and selfishness put one's own *wants* first at the expense of needs.

A culture of hyper-communication, overdrive and huge workloads from which there is little or no respite can create a kind of vortex that is very hard to get out of. Leaders can easily find themselves sucked into this vortex, telling themselves that, 'once this next project or few months is past, things will *definitely* settle down'.

Of course, this rarely ever happens. No sooner has the current urgent priority passed, than the next one (or several!) hits the priority list. It can be very difficult to get out of the vortex. For leaders who are very personally invested in their work (e.g. as an entrepreneur), highly driven and ambitious (e.g. have very high expectations of themselves) or who feel out of their depth with a lack of support around them, this is a big issue. Many new leaders find themselves in such a situation. Leading ourselves, and investing in our own mental health, is key.

The common metaphor of filling a jar with rocks, pebbles, sand and water applies well here. The rocks are our major priorities, then the pebbles are lesser priorities, then the sand, and so on all the way to the water or minutia. The rocks are not just major work priorities. They also include the other important parts of your life such as close relationships and time for self-care. You want to make sure your rocks are in the jar first, then the pebbles can fit in around them, followed by the sand that fills the spaces, and finally the water. You don't want the water and sand in the jar first because the rocks won't be able to fit in. When we're in overdrive we often fixate on busy work and minutia, making it very difficult to ensure those rocks are in the jar and we're prioritizing them. In fact, we can forget what our rocks are or that they even exist!

If you stand back and look at your life, do you find that, in the name of productivity and efficiency, you fill every spare minute with checking emails and notifications until you have conditioned yourself into mindlessly scrolling whether you need to or not? This is like filling the jar with sand and water. A simple way to check this is to run a 'mini audit' on yourself at the end of each day: what percentage of the day did I spend attending to rocks versus sand and water? We innately know what is and is not important to us. No one else (not even our partner!) can tell us what our rocks are. The tricky bit, however, can be in keeping these rocks clear and fresh in our daily lives, so they are not pushed into the background.

Focus Question 1: Ask yourself, what is, ultimately, most important in my life? Keeping a question like this firmly in view, and actually giving it the time it deserves, is a key skill for any leader. Stop for a moment, stand back from yourself and, with a quiet but caring attitude, look at what you see. If you are happy with what you observe then all is well and you can get back to what you were doing before. If you see things that are out of place, significant stress, grumbling dissatisfaction and frenetic but aimless actions then stop and give yourself a little breathing space. What are the main priorities for you (rocks), and what are the secondary priorities (pebbles)? Do you need to take anything of lesser importance out of the jar to make space for the things that are really important? And have you neglected self-care as one of your main priorities? What do you need to do to re-prioritize self-care, as well as attending to your other rocks (major priorities)?

If we have established an attitude that self-care is not selfish then the next obvious thing to consider is how we best care for the self, so let us turn our attention now to self-replenishment.

Self-replenishment

As a leader, you probably give a lot of yourself to the job and the people around you. It is therefore critically important to take time to renew yourself. It would be ridiculous to run a business based on delivering parcels but think that keeping the delivery vans serviced and in good running order was an expensive indulgence. It may seem an unprofitable use of time to take the van off the road for a service, but that is exactly what is required to keep them running reliably. Why would we care for machines like delivery vans more than we care for human beings?

As mentioned in Chapter 4, if we don't take time to replenish ourselves, our well will soon run dry, making it hard for anyone to draw from it. Lifestyle is of central importance. Unfortunately, research shows that the more addicted we are to technology like smartphones then the more likely we are sacrifice other things related to health, like physical exercise or sleep.[3,4,5]

When tired and working in a sedentary work environment we often get into a cycle of increasing tiredness by being even more sedentary in our leisure time when we actually need to increase our energy by regularly doing some *physical exercise*. Physical exercise, particularly aerobic exercise, helps to prevent depression and is a mental health intervention in itself.[6,7] Replenishing ourselves also means eating a healthy *diet*. When stressed we often reach for comfort food rather than healthy food. This creates an immediate pleasure hit but then has a rebound negative impact on energy and mood. A healthy diet is also important preventively and therapeutically for mental health.[8] We may also be sacrificing *sleep* or have got into an irregular sleep pattern, especially if we are using devices like smartphones before bed and during the night. This impairs concentration and performance and is a significant risk factor for depression. Poor sleep and stress can be compounded by self-medicating with *excessive alcohol* or other *substances*. We may not be finding time for *relationships* and social activities with friends or family. Lastly, we may not be taking time for the *leisure activities* that replenish, inspire or energize us including meditation, creative or community-based activities. There may be other things you can think of that enhance your wellbeing.

The problem is that doing things that deplete us and ignoring the activities that replenish us soon gets us into a negative spiral of illbeing. They have an additive effect — like adding weights that drag us down while we are trying to tread water on the surface.

Equally, making one healthy change at a time, and then gradually adding another, can move us into an upward spiral of wellbeing. By attending to our basic elements of wellbeing, we build up our resources so we're better placed to navigate the demands on our attention that we face as leaders. To use the metaphor of treading water, it's like dropping the weights and holding on to things that give us buoyancy. In psychology, this is known as the *conservation of resources* theory of managing stress and is one of the most well-researched and widely used approaches to understanding human resilience.[9] By identifying our own core elements of wellbeing, we are enhancing our own reserves, which places us in a much better position to engage with the complex human interactions that go with leadership.

Practical experiment 1: Taking time for self-care

Begin by giving yourself a global rating out of ten over the preceding week for each of the following: energy, mood, engagement and enthusiasm. Now, this experiment is about you reflecting on four wellbeing-related priorities that are important to you but in need of a bit of work. Clarify in your own mind what those four are and write yourself a SMART goal (specific, measurable, achievable, realistic and time-bound) related to each of these priorities. Put the goals in order from easiest to toughest and make a contract with yourself that you will institute one new goal per week over the next four weeks, starting with the easiest. The goals don't have to be momentous or onerous, but just things that are steps towards a healthier direction for you. Start with implementing your first goal in the first week. Each week introduce the next goal and maintain the preceding week's goals so that by the end of four weeks you have made and are maintaining four healthier behaviours. At the outset, you may find it helpful to tell someone else such as your partner or health professional about your goals. That will make you more accountable. At the end of the fourth week revisit your global ratings for energy, mood, engagement and enthusiasm. See what you notice.

Functional reserve: The art of staying out of crisis

There are many business principles that have been brought into modern medicine to good effect aimed at improving quality of care and reducing clinical errors. But medicine, being all about health, also has some principles that are applicable to business and the workplace. One such principle is *functional reserve.*

Functional reserve is a medical term. It denotes the reserve a tissue or organ has between its basal physiological functioning and its capacity to increase function in situations of higher demands. So, for example, if a person lost 10 per cent of kidney function because they had an acute illness it would have no measurable or material effect on their health. From a kidney perspective, they wouldn't even know. There is plenty of kidney function in reserve to more than cope. If that person lost a kidney due to injury or cancer — i.e. a 50 per cent drop in kidney function — it would still make no discernible difference to their health because the remaining kidney has plenty of capacity to fulfil all necessary kidney functions. If, however, the remaining kidney also lost half of its function, meaning that there was only 25 per cent of original kidney function remaining, then blood tests may show changes and the person might start to experience some symptoms because the remaining 25 per cent is not enough to fully do everything the kidney needs to do. By this stage there would be measurable changes in the blood, symptoms in the body and the person would not feel like they were in optimum health. An acute illness that leads to a 10 per cent further drop in kidney function could easily temporarily put the system into crisis. If the person permanently loses another 10 per cent, so they only have 15 per cent remaining, then they would be in kidney failure and would need significant medical intervention to continue living. The message is that nature, in its infinite wisdom, is generally extremely generous. In the normal scheme of things, the kidney, and all other bodily organs, have plenty in reserve so that we can function healthily and be resilient to challenges.

Kidney physiology may or may not be interesting to you, and you are probably wondering what it has got to do with leadership and wellbeing. Well, let's consider the principle of functional reserve but in relation to life and work. It has become an entrenched line of thinking that having excess capacity is waste and therefore needs to be cut to the minimum so that we can be optimally efficient. Technology has facilitated enormously the march to fill every minute of time and to cut margins to an extreme. It looks efficient and profitable on the surface, but it may not be such a good policy if it leaves the individual or workplace perpetually on the edge of crisis. We may not need 75 per cent functional reserve like the kidney, but we may need a lot more than the 1 per cent we are probably allowing ourselves.

For example, from an individual perspective, if you fill every spare minute in your calendar then you have no functional reserve for when an unexpected situation occurs. Suddenly, the workflow and deadlines you had previously planned are totally disrupted and events take on a pressured and perhaps chaotic air. Similarly, if you are working in such a way that you are expending energy at near capacity then there is little energy in reserve if demands go up a notch and you need to put your foot on the accelerator. Suddenly, you feel exhausted, overwhelmed and want to run and hide. Likewise, if you are having your emotional reserves drawn on at near capacity each working day then you may have little left to draw on when you get home. Then if your partner or child presents a concern to you or asks for some time and attention you feel suddenly overwhelmed and either snap and get angry, or want to retreat to the bottle or the television. Financially, if you have maximized debt to the point where you are only just able to comfortably cover it then you have little in reserve if circumstances change. Suddenly, interest rates go up, or your pay or hours are cut, and then you find yourself on the edge of a financial crisis. If you are experiencing such things, then you may well be leaving little or no functional reserve in the way you live, work or plan your finances. Hence it only takes little shocks to put you into crisis mode. There are many other examples that can be given, but you will notice this by its effects on your stress levels, behaviour and related symptoms.

As a leader, how much functional reserve do you leave in the systems and work practices you oversee? For example, if you set a deadline that requires everyone to be under pressure and for everything to go to plan without hitches then the chances are that everyone will be rushed, the unexpected inevitably happens and the final product is suboptimal. Airline timetables can have so little space in them that it only takes a relatively little shock — a plane is delayed for some relatively minor reason — and the whole system is put into crisis with a series of widespread and far-reaching knock-on effects. The system never catches up until it is reset the next day. In a business, has the profit margin been so eaten away to the extent that it only takes small and unexpected challenges to make the business unprofitable? Has a business's growth and level of debt been increased to the maximum capacity of its ability to service that debt based on the assumption that things like interest rates will keep going as expected? Just consider how many businesses have gone under because of the effects of rising interest rates and inflation post-COVID. How many staff has a business employed to do a certain amount of work? Only barely enough? If so, then one may find that, in times of challenge or increased demand, absenteeism, reduced motivation and resignations are the result and the whole system falls into crisis. Then an enormous amount of time and energy is spent covering for missing colleagues and the business must train new people to take their positions. Again, there are many other examples that can be given, but the energy and stress expended in dealing with these largely self-inflicted crises, as well as the errors that arise from them, will be far more than the apparent loss associated with building in a little more space into timetables, budgets and workforces. Working without the right amount of functional reserve is a false sense of economy. It's a mistake that repeats itself again and again on small and large scales.

Functional reserve is not waste. It's the basis upon which health, resilience and the ability to cope with challenges are based. The other factor to consider is that when we are constantly squeezed for time and energy, and when the mind is agitated and concerned, then it impairs focus, creativity and decision making.[10] This means that, through distraction and cognitive exhaustion, errors increase while innovation, quality and standards are impaired. Avoiding an overfull or cluttered diary or environment also reflects itself in a less cluttered mind. Evidence shows that this allows for greater clarity and top-down control of decisions and actions.[11]

You may not need to factor in 75 per cent functional reserve like the kidney, but the chances are, whether an individual or an organization, you would do well to factor in a little more reserve into the system than you currently do. You will not only conserve a lot of energy and stress but you will be able to step out of the repetitive cycle of so frequently going in and out of crisis.

Focus Question 2: How much functional reserve do you build into your life? This might reveal itself in how much white space you keep in your calendar, how much of the time you feel on the edge of your energy reserves, how emotionally depleted you feel, or how financially stretched you feel. What are the effects on your mind, emotions and body of being in this state on a regular basis? Is it serving you well? Can you increase the amount of functional reserve by doing things like keeping more white space in the calendar for when the unexpected happens? Can you hurry less and conserve more physical and emotional energy? Can you make financial decisions in such a way that you only take on debt that you can comfortably cope with even if the financial or work situations change? Do you need to build in more than the minimal amount of self-renewal and leisure time that you are currently allowing yourself?

Practical experiment 2: Increase your functional reserve

You might find it helpful to practise a mindfulness exercise to help you settle and focus before doing a reflective exercise like this. Once you are settled, based on your reflections on the questions above, prioritize areas of your life where you need to build in more functional reserve. Estimate how much reserve you currently have in those areas and formulate a new and more sustainable level of functional reserve. Formulate a plan about when and how you will instigate those changes. Having implemented them, see what the effects are after one week and then one month.

You can increase your functional reserve by reducing the workload and number of commitments you have, a bit like releasing some of the water from an overfull dam so that it still has the capacity to deal with an unexpected deluge should one happen. There is another option as well. You can increase your functional reserve by increasing your capacity to meet demands. That's a bit like increasing the storage capacity of a dam by having its walls extended to be able to hold more water. That not only means that there is more in reserve for times of drought, but it also means that an unexpected deluge won't put such a strain on the dam wall that it breaks. Increasing capacity is not about simply working harder, as if using more adrenaline will solve our problems. As we have considered, stress will only increase performance to a point before wellbeing and performance both start to suffer. Increasing capacity has more to do with working smarter — greater efficiency, better prioritizing, better focus and less distraction, using less energy to provide more output. Mindfulness-based techniques can be enormously helpful in this regard, but we also should not ignore the underlying attitudes and systemic issues that deplete our reserves and need to be addressed.

The always-on work culture

An always-on work culture can really have an impact on leaders themselves. This is a big issue and is, rightly, receiving growing recognition as organizations take the issues of stress, burnout and mental ill-health more seriously. Leaders certainly are — or need to be — focused on these issues. A survey by Deloitte found that nearly 70 per cent of executives were thinking about leaving their current jobs and moving to workplaces that cared more for their employees' wellbeing, and 57 per cent of non-managerial employees wanted to leave for similar reasons.[12]

Just like the other issues we've unpacked above, there is a growing body of scientific research exploring the impacts of always-on working and tech-dependence on leaders' mental health and wellbeing. One large area of focus is the impact of tech use for work on people's work–life balance. Having blocks of downtime each night, and also during the day, is critical for reducing cognitive load and sustaining ourselves. In these periods of downtime, we are typically engaged in tasks other than work (e.g. domestic tasks, caring for children, exercising, socializing or doing something creative). In order for this downtime to benefit us, it needs to be not just physical disengagement from work (e.g. being out of the office), but also mental disengagement. Much of the time you can be, and probably are, physically at home but mentally still at work. And this is where the rubber hits the road.

Constant connectivity via devices have made it very, very difficult for these pockets of downtime to actually be downtime. We might be physically in a restaurant, at the gym or out for a walk. But our ever-present device keeps our mind regularly connected to and preoccupied about our work. One study interviewed knowledge professionals about the flexibility that technology brings.[13] Strikingly, these researchers uncovered what they called a 'paradox of autonomy': while constant work-connectivity made people *think* they have greater autonomy and flexibility to work at times and in places that suit them, in practice, it had the opposite effect. The professionals felt increasingly bound and controlled as they sensed a growing social pressure to respond quickly, and at any time, to work issues because this had become the norm across the business. The initial appeal of the apparent freedom to respond anywhere and at any time, quickly turns into the tyranny of expectation to respond everywhere and always.

There is now a large body of research showing that this way of living and working is bad for our capacity to sustain ourselves. Studies have shown that when professionals use their smartphones to work at night, this negatively impacts the quality of sleep and lowers their work engagement the next day.[14] A recent study of Dutch employees found that people's work-related device use after hours was linked to greater work–family conflict.[15] Another study followed US HR professionals over six working days and found that technology demands (specifically email demands) lead to greater work stress and fuelled work–family conflict.[16] This effect was amplified in people who reported chronically lower levels of self-regulation (i.e. the capacity to regulate reactions to situations and sustain focus on valued tasks). So it seems that this inability to switch-off harms not only our own mental health and ability to recharge, but also our closest and most important relationships.[17] As we've discussed, these so-called 'downtime' activities are, for most people, important and highly valued (e.g. spending time with children, your partner, getting into nature, doing exercise, etc.). If we're not giving our full attention while we're doing these things, we're unwittingly sacrificing our rocks and giving preference to sand and water instead.

Maintaining balance and wellbeing in a work-from-home world

One of the biggest recent changes in the way work gets done is the rapid shift, triggered by COVID, to work from home (WFH). If WFH is done well it can enhance our wellbeing, but if done poorly it will have the opposite effect. Although the advantages of convenience and reduced commuting are generally welcome, downsides like turning the home into an always-on workplace mean that work has the potential to impact our personal life in a way it never had before.

During COVID-19 lockdowns, there was generally little else we could do, so, 'why not just check the emails again!' We were often so fused to our technology that we never let it out of our reach, even when we could. As a result, for many people, WFH has meant working longer hours rather than fewer, as well as finding it hard to switch off, particularly if you don't have a high level of psychological detachment (i.e. an ability to let go), or other pressing calls on your time and energy taking you away from work (e.g. children, social commitments, sport, etc.). Now COVID-19 lockdowns are a thing of the past, but many of the unhelpful habits and work practices are not. We're always-on in a way we never were before and this affects us personally in a variety of ways. Our home life impacts work and work impacts personal life.

COVID-19 triggered some important studies on WFH impacts. This research found that for people in leadership and management positions, greater collaboration via digital platforms induced technostress due to the cognitive demands needed to connect effectively with staff online versus face to face. This led to increased psychological strain, technology exhaustion and decreased wellbeing. However, those with previous WFH experience negotiated technostress better, perhaps because they had already set reasonable boundaries.[18] In other research, it was found that the factors associated with decreased physical and mental wellbeing due to WFH were reduced physical exercise, unhealthy food intake, lack of meaningful communication with co-workers, negotiating children at home and their home-schooling, uncontrolled distractions while working, adjusted and sometimes unstructured work hours, poor workstation set-up and dissatisfaction with the indoor workspace environment.[19]

There are other interesting findings from research on the impact of family–work conflict. [20] This research found that employees' family–work conflict and social isolation are associated with less productivity and work engagement, but greater self-leadership and autonomy. A study explored the effects on employees' psychological wellbeing (measured in terms of stress and happiness), productivity and engagement of three 'stress relievers' of the WFH environment. These relievers were company support, supervisor's trust in the employee, and work–life balance. Of the three stress relievers, work–life balance was the only one that significantly improved psychological wellbeing, and happiness improved productivity. The researchers concluded that the '... findings provide evidence that management's maintenance of a healthy work–life balance for colleagues when they are working from home is important for supporting their psychosocial wellbeing and in turn upholding their work productivity.' [21]

All of the above suggests that WFH can undermine our wellbeing when work becomes fused with our personal life. But if it is done well, there are benefits in terms of wellbeing and balance. Some strategies for maintaining balance during WFH include how we structure our time at home and the boundaries we set. This requires a level of self-discipline while we establish these WFH practices. For example, schedule breaks and reasonable start and finish work times just as you would at your workplace. Then be proactive in allocating the time you are saving from commuting and allocate it to activities that promote wellbeing and replenish you. Create separate environments for work and personal life. For example, have a workspace or office, and when you finish work, remove yourself from that space and close the door behind you.

All of the above will be easier if you give yourself a five- or ten-minute mindfulness meditation break or go for a walk in the fresh air so that you mentally leave the work behind you as well as physically removing yourself from the home office. A survey of a diverse range of employees across 46 organizations found that although psychological detachment, sleep, stress, social support, work–life balance and productivity declined as a result of WFH, psychological detachment was a positive influence on stress and sleep and thereby supported productivity. Furthermore, social support significantly helps participants maintain work–life balance.[22] So, be sure to spend a good proportion of that extra time you now have on your hands with the important people in your life. We explore these issues more fully in practical experiment 3 below.

Practical experiment 3

Consider your home life. How does your use of devices (including for work) impact your home life? What key relationships or activities does it disrupt? Experiment with one of the following three domains of device disruption at home:

1) Meals. What role do devices/screens play in your mealtimes at home? What is the impact of this on the quality of connection and sharing with your family, partner or housemates? For one week, make a commitment to have no devices present during meals. Fully connect with the food you're eating. Connect fully with those you are eating with. Notice the impact.

2) Downtime. How many hours do you spend on a screen during periods of downtime? For one week try substituting this screen downtime with something tactile and physical. Try taking up a hobby such as drawing, painting, sport or music. Or it could be as simple as going for a light walk or reading a real (i.e. printed) book. Notice the impact after one week.

3) Sleep. For one week try committing to not checking a device within one hour of going to sleep and not having your mobile device within reach when you go to bed. To make this task easier, choose a healthier alternative. Examples are a light walk (which also helps with digestion before sleep), listening to some music (though if it's via your smartphone, you'll likely become perilously close to scrolling through social media), or reading a book that really interests and engages you (this gives you some of the reward and satisfaction your device would, without the sleep-damaging side-effects).

Successively work your way through these three domains and run the experiment for one week. Make a note of the impacts. Keep doing it if you notice useful effects from it.

The disrupted leader

Aside from these work–life impacts, there are also more immediate effects of intensive tech-use dependence for work. One issue that has been explored in several studies are so-called 'work interruptions' that interrupt the flow of complex tasks. These interruptions might be a colleague dropping into your office unannounced to ask you a question, breaking your flow of concentration on an important piece of work. Much more common, of course, is the arrival of an email or message via a collaboration app, which, if we have our notifications always on, pops up on-screen and to which we unconsciously and compulsively react to. Instead of staying in the flow of what we were doing, we jump to the new task until another one pops up, and then another, and another, until we have many tabs open and many jobs half done.

Studies have begun to look at the impacts of these *micro-disruptions* on our performance, satisfaction and engagement at work. One study found that there was an increased error rate of 28 per cent when a task was interrupted by a text message notification, even if the person didn't respond to it.[23] Consider the implications for occupations where such errors can have major implications, such as driving, air traffic control and healthcare.

Another study found that each interruption led to an average 64 seconds of lost productivity, which, considering the frequency of such interruptions, added up to 8.5 hours of lost productivity in the working week.[24] That's the equivalent of more than one full work day lost each week! Yet another study followed US employees over three weeks at work, looking at the frequency of interruptions and how this impacted their work satisfaction.[25] The researchers found that, over time, these interruptions degraded people's job satisfaction by depleting their energy and vitality. Interestingly, this study found that, at the same time, these work interruptions enhanced a sense of 'belongingness', due to the incidental social interactions that often come with disruptions. However, the overall effect in this study was a lowering of job satisfaction.

While these challenges are by no means new, we do not see them disappearing into the rear-view mirror anytime soon. If anything, the impacts of tech-mediated collaboration on these important areas of leadership continue to grow and their impacts compound. This is especially so as AI becomes ever more embedded in the way work gets done, teams collaborate, and services and goods are delivered. One of the unfortunate things about the way organizations approach new technology is that it often gets universally and enthusiastically adopted before it has proven its benefits and its negative effects have been delineated. We can't expect the people who make and market such technologies to measure, let alone be interested in, their downsides because that doesn't sell the product. We need to adopt a more cautious and questioning attitude and have our ears and eyes open to what the evidence from research and personal experience is telling us.

Practical experiment 4

Consider how you arrange your workspace in terms of disruptions and distractions. What kinds of auto-prompts do you have switched on and consider which ones you can turn off (e.g. new emails, new Slack and Teams messages, other communications platforms and similar prompts on your phone). Try turning these interrupting technologies off for one week and assess the impacts. Also consider how you arrange your workflow. You can 'chunk' or 'compartmentalize' your time by diarizing specific blocks of time in the day to check and respond to messages (e.g. 10 a.m., 2 p.m. and 4 p.m.) for 30 minutes each. Carve out other uninterrupted blocks of time for 'deep work', i.e. those complex planning, creative or writing activities that require more focus and longer blocks of time. Early in the day, while the mind is still relatively fresh, is a good time for deep work. At the end of the week, assess how you feel in terms of energy, focus and mental balance, as well as in terms of productivity.

Social media is not always so sociable

These days, social media is seen by many as being indispensable in personal life and essential to running an effective business. It can certainly have its uses if it is used well, but if not, then it can cause a number of problems, including for our wellbeing. Technology and social media can affect us in a variety of ways, which can have secondary impacts on how we see others and interact with them. It also has a potentially distorting effect on how we see ourselves.

An interesting impact of social media is that it seems to increase a preoccupation with oneself. So much of its focus is on 'me', my 'self-image', how others see 'me', or how we want them to see 'me'. This has a substantial negative impact on mental health. One study found that among young adults who use social media the most, social media use increased threefold the risk of depression compared to those who use it the least.[26] Other studies have found that the more a person uses *visual* forms of social media in particular, the more narcissistic the person tends to become.[27] The constant focus for the mind is on social comparison and 'me', 'am I being noticed?', and 'what people think about me', and 'are people thinking about me?' This does ourselves and our self-esteem little good. As one evidence-based review pointed out, '... social network sites benefit their users when they are used to make meaningful social connections and harm their users through pitfalls such as isolation and social comparison when they are not.'[28] Unfortunately, social media tends towards cultivating self-obsessed, opinionated, in-groups/out-groups and reactive aspects of human nature. The mind is increasingly being unconsciously shaped by misinformation and the algorithms that someone else has determined for you. Consuming time by interacting with people in this virtual way means that we are not finding time for interacting in a more direct and human way.

How do these impacts show up for leaders? The bottom line is that these impacts are barely understood. Much more research is needed to better understand how and when the social online world impacts the ways in which leaders present and project themselves among those they lead and the wider community. Of course, there are easy examples that capture everyone's attention. Donald Trump. Elon Musk. Jeff Bezos. But what about for 'everyday' leaders without that kind of profile? In a hyper-networked world, there is always the temptation as a leader to put yourself further and further out on a limb on social media, because this gets attention. Leaders tread a fine line here, using social media to promote their organization's work, share their thoughts on issues and stay connected with their network. But they also need to use it judiciously, and always with awareness of how easily and quickly your professional identity can be torn apart if you get yourself into the wrong place at the wrong time.

The leader's way: Balance

Balance is a crucial aspect of wellbeing and functioning well. With the addictive, pervasive and attention-monopolizing nature of a lot of the information technology we use, balance is a hard commodity to find unless we become the masters of technology rather than its servants. Balance doesn't only apply to our use of technology but also to finding the right balance in other aspects of life related to wellbeing, such as lifestyle, relationships and leisure time.

The leader who is aware and a master of themselves is also a positive influence on those around them. Research shows that a leader, just by virtue of being more mindful, is not only more balanced in themselves but also influences teams to display better work–life balance.[29] The leader who is not a master of themselves is easily pushed around, whether it be consciously or unconsciously, by the influences around them regardless of whether those influences are useful, healthy or not. This is not a precedent we want to set for a work environment.

One factor associated with better emotional health that comes up again and again in psychological research is psychological detachment. In acceptance and commitment therapy (ACT) they sometimes call this defusion. When we are psychologically attached to something — say, an opinion, desire or a prized possession — we can't let it go even if we need to. We get 'fused' with it, and we have all observed the effect this has on our mind, emotions, words and behaviour. It fixates our attention on it, making it harder to engage with whatever else is going on around us. You may have noticed that, in the middle of the night, thoughts and concerns related to work come into your field of awareness and you can't seem to leave them alone. To be detached, to be able to let go, to 'de-fuse' from it takes awareness and effort but if we cultivate that ability — for example, through the regular practice of meditation — then it stands us in good stead. Detachment makes it easier for us to switch on when we need to but, importantly, to switch off from work when we need to. Work–life balance becomes a whole lot easier then.

Here are some other personal practices and policy recommendations to help foster personal and workplace balance.

Three personal practices

Practice 1: Make time for self-renewal regularly.

Choose the few key things in life that energize, inspire, recharge your batteries or give greater meaning to your life. These things could be connecting with family or friends, physical exercise, meditation, getting out into nature, a creative pursuit or the spiritual/philosophical aspects of life. The point is, make sure you carve out time regularly to do those things. Put it in your calendar or diary if you need to, but make sure those things are prioritized as a part of your day, week and year.

Practice 2: Keep enough functional reserve in your life.

Make this a part of how you organize your working and personal life. For example, keep some white space in your calendar or diary so that if on any given day something unexpected arises you have some space to allow for it. When travelling, allow a generous enough amount of time so that you minimize rushing. If the trip is slower than expected then you won't be stressed about it and if you arrive a little early then you have time to smell the roses, enjoy the view and settle yourself so that you are in a good mental space for what comes next. If you have a project, then don't cut the deadline to the bone but make it generous enough that you have contingency for the unexpected. You likely can finish ahead of the deadline, and then take time to refine, correct or polish before completion. Avoid pushing your finances or level of debt to their limit assuming that financial conditions will remain as they are, because they won't. That way, if things take an unexpected downturn, you won't be under undue strain, but if they go better than expected then you have a surplus to enjoy.

Practice 3: Put the rocks in first.

Consider your response to Focus Question 1 relating to your priorities in life. What are your most important priorities in life (the rocks) and what are the secondary priorities (the pebbles)? Don't worry about the other busywork and lesser priorities (the sand and water) because they will fit in around the rocks and pebbles. Now, sit down and reflect on whether you have made space for the rocks and, if not, how you will make space for them. Mentally empty the jar if you need to and start again with an open mind. How will you ensure those things that are most important to you are given their rightful place in your life? Then consider what pebbles or lesser priorities are. How many of them can you or do you need to make space for? Maybe not everything you want will fit in the jar so make a decision about what is most important for you (and the other important people in your life) right now and leave the others for another day or another phase of your life. You might like to map it out on a piece of paper. Take your time, and when you have mapped it out, sit with it for a day or two and look at it again. Are there any changes or further considerations you need to allow for? When you feel settled in what you have come up with, take steps to implement what you have written. Maybe there aren't many changes you need to make because you already have your rocks in place, or maybe there are a number of changes you need to make. So be it. It may be a challenge at first but you will be far better off in the long run if you get the basic foundations of your life in place. Please avoid rushing reflective processes like this one. Do it when you have some space, peace and quiet.

Three policy recommendations

» *Recommendation 1: Ensure that wellbeing is a workplace priority.* If you are a leader then you may well have the capacity to be an instigator or advocate for ensuring that the wellbeing of the people in your team or organization is a priority. Workplace wellbeing programs might seem to be an expense in terms of time or money but if the happiness and wellbeing of the people you work with is supported then it will return the investment many times over. You will also have the added bonus of working in a happier workplace where people are more enthusiastic about coming to work. Choosing what kinds of programs and interventions to introduce, and choosing the right people to deliver them, are important choices so please don't rush those decisions. Don't just assume that throwing money at anyone who approaches you wanting to deliver something will have the desired outcome. Recommendations from people you respect, as well as asking for evidence to back up people's claims, are a good place to start.

» *Recommendation 2: Make functional reserve a key consideration in all planning and policy decisions.* As for the individual, so for the organization. Whether it is in relation to staffing, scheduling, deadlines, financial decisions or anything else, keep enough space available to allow for unexpected contingencies so that you will improve the quality of your work and keep yourself and your organization out of crisis mode.

» *Recommendation 3: Put the rocks in first.* Much was said about this in Chapter 3 on priorities, but from a wellbeing perspective also, let planning decisions prioritize the most major priorities first. The same reflective questions that you have put to yourself can be put to the organization and people in senior management positions. Are the organization's most important priorities being attended to or is their importance being marginalized amid the minutia and busywork?

Summary

The research on these issues is rapidly unfolding, uncovering new and important insights in how we interact with technology, and the impacts of this on our wellbeing and capacity to lead. In this chapter we have highlighted a few areas where we see these impacts showing up most clearly from a personal perspective. Having explored some factors influencing wellbeing — like self-care, lifestyle, functional reserve and the need for balance — hopefully you are better motivated and equipped to make necessary health changes in your life. Rather than just highlighting the problem, our intention is also to explore how organizations and leaders can manage these challenges: taking the best of what technology brings, without sacrificing ourselves or those we care about in the process. In the next chapter on 'Progress' we summarize key messages and tips from the book and provide practical guidance for you as a leader, and your leadership team, in building your capability to navigate these challenges.

Chapter 6

Progress

As we draw together the key takeaways from this book, we invite you to reflect on how you are tracking on the key issues and skills we have discussed. In this chapter we provide a process for doing this reflection through two different lenses. The first is at a leadership team level. We provide a suggested approach for a leader taking their core senior leadership team through a 'leadership audit', so that they are focused on the right things. We structure this using the four Ps from previous chapters (Purpose, Priorities, People and Personal). The second lens we offer is at a personal level. That is, you as an individual leader. To do this, we draw on the four core leadership attributes we have outlined in 'The Leader's Way' sections of the preceding chapters: authenticity, awareness, openness and balance. We provide a set of reflective questions linked to each of these four attributes for you to consider and then identify meaningful actions you will take.

Leadership team capabilities for an always-on world

In almost every organization, business, division or team, the leader does not operate alone. As history shows us, leaders who operate alone (e.g. who avoid conflicting advice, countervailing viewpoints or who hold key information too tightly) tend to make poor decisions and be unsuccessful. As a leader, you want to be alive to the leadership priorities and capacities not just of yourself, but also of your core group of senior colleagues and leaders.

In this section we offer a simple process for auditing you and your core leadership team so that you are focused on the right things. As with everything in this book, our focus is on leadership teams grappling with leading in a hyperactive, often-distracted, information-saturated environment — whether you are a CEO leading an executive team, a project executive leading teams of project directors or a part of any other intact leadership team. This section is for leadership teams who, although they might feel they are performing well, are nevertheless grappling with being overloaded or perhaps overrun with multiple and conflicting priorities. It is also for leadership teams who want to consolidate and clarify the capabilities they need to lead well in a complex operating environment.

Below we provide a simple, four-step method to help your leadership team clarify where their strengths are, and what areas need development. We suggest you use these questions with your leadership team as a 'leadership audit' and conversation starter, leading to actions and initiatives that address your collective weaknesses and reinforce your collective strengths. Based on our work with various intact leadership teams, our preference is to make this exercise a dialectic one, where your team uses the dialectic exercise in Chapter 4 to build shared understanding, identify points of friction, and gain clarity and alignment on what your priorities are as a team.

The leadership 'diagnostic' industry (i.e. surveys, quantitative analyses and reports) is a multimillion-dollar business. While diagnostic tools have their place, our experience is that a) they are often needlessly complicated and b) even when they are accessible, they only deliver insight when used as a springboard for a dialectic conversation. Leadership teams and HR professionals can often hide behind diagnostics with a false sense of clarity on where they are at as a team, without addressing the nuances, dynamics and underlying issues that might be holding the team back. Our general preference is to jump straight into the dialectic and trust that, when facilitated well, the insights and priorities will emerge from an engaging, honest but respectful conversation.

There are four broad steps we suggest you take. Of course, you may want to design something different, cherry-picking elements of what we present below and repurposing it for your needs. Having said that, we find that these four steps tend to work well in most leadership teams. The core of what we outline below is based on the four 'Ps' critical to leaders and teams of leaders remaining effective and relevant in times of flux and change. The Ps are also critical for leaders keeping their teams and people focused on the right things, consistently over time. Above all else, they are key to leading any organization for sustained success (and avoiding being taken out in a competitive and uncertain environment).

Step 1: Bullseye

First up, we have found that teams often find it helpful to 'kick the tyres' on the four Ps. That is, have a brief discussion first up about *why* the Ps matter to you as a team, which of the Ps you see as most valuable, and why. Checking-in at the beginning can really help build engagement and clarity within your leadership team as to which of these Ps may be most important and which less so.

You then move into a high-level audit of how the leadership team is performing on each of the Ps. You can use the bullseye diagram below as a conversation starter here. The leadership team can ask itself: 'Which elements are we doing well on as a leadership team? How do we score, and what broad factors are driving our scores?' If you want to add some rigour to this audit, you can run a quick anonymous survey among staff within the business or identify a selection of staff to provide anonymous feedback before engaging on the bullseye.

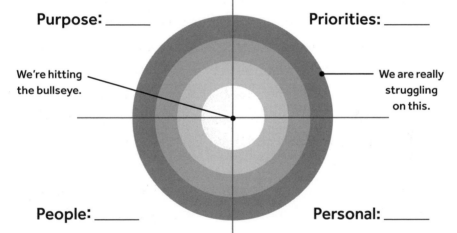

We are clear on the needs we exist to serve, and the values that deliver this. Our purpose is clearly reflected in the decisions we take as a leadership team and is well integrated across our team/organization.

Purpose: _____

We are consistently focused on the right strategic issues. We are good at stepping back and seeing the bigger picture, but can also 'seize the moment' when we need to move fast. As a leadership team, we engage with each other with full attention, non-reactivity and honesty.

Priorities: _____

We're hitting the bullseye.

We are really struggling on this.

People: _____

As a leadership team, we embody qualities of openness, interpersonal honesty and presence when we engage with each other and those we lead.

Personal: _____

As a leadership team, we have the appropriate amount of 'functional reserve'. We look after our own wellbeing and resilience, so that we can sustain ourselves in our leadership role. We look out for each other. We role model self-care among those we lead.

Step 2: Drill down

Having conducted a brief, high-level audit of where your leadership is on the bullseye (Step 1), you can now drill down into the responses and corroborate these against the questions we've detailed in previous chapters and also listed below, with some minor variations. The idea is that you are now testing your initial responses (from Step 1) against these additional questions. We find that Step 2 often unearths additional issues that Step 1 does not capture.

For this exercise, we generally recommend breaking your leadership team into smaller groups to tackle each block of questions. To focus your team's attention, you might wish to first identify the one or two most strategically important and relevant questions for your leadership team. For example, under 'Purpose', it might be that you already have an organizational purpose and values but how you engage and communicate this needs work, or how you 'translate' these for your specific business area might need attention and consideration. Or, as another example, under 'People', your leadership team might decide that the organization has an engaged staff, but that a really important issue is that people do not feel confident asking questions or challenging assumptions and decisions, and that this is impacting the quality of decisions made. This would then be your focus for assessing the 'People' dimension. As a third example, under 'Personal', you might decide that you as a leadership team are quite good at supporting each other, but that there is a culture within the team (and perhaps the wider organization) that is not supportive enough of people stepping forward and asking for help when they are struggling. As a result, people are often not looking after their own personal needs and are burning out. This would then be one of your areas of focus in assessing the 'Personal' dimension.

Purpose

» What is the core need or needs we exist to serve?

» Do we have a clear statement of purpose, values and behaviours that reflect these needs?

» How might we ensure that our purpose and values are shared and co-owned across the organization?

» How authentic are we being (i.e. to what extent does our stated purpose reflect our organization's actual reason for being)?

» How effectively are we communicating purpose?

» How consistently do our behaviours as leaders embody our stated purpose and values?

Priorities

» How clear are we about our most important strategic challenges?

» To what extent are we focusing on the right issues at the right time (versus being distracted or derailed by non-strategically important issues)?

» In general, how effective is our balance between moving forward, planning and making decisions (i.e. convergent thinking), versus unpacking, teasing apart and trying to understand the problems and priorities we face (i.e. divergent thinking)?

» How responsive, non-reactive and balanced are we in discussing the difficult but important strategic questions we face?

People

» How engaged and driven are our staff to deliver for the organization?

» How aligned are our staff behind our purpose and values?

» How well do we listen to, engage and communicate with our people?

» How safe and supported do our people feel to ask questions, challenge assumptions and raise concerns?

» What kind of culture have we created as an organization? What are its core features and hallmarks compared with other organizations in our industry?

» How close to our ideal is our current work culture? What issues do we need to focus on to build the organizational culture we want?

Personal

» How well are we, as a leadership team, looking after our own personal needs?

» How well are we supporting each other, as leaders and as people?

» How much does our own internal culture (i.e. within our leadership team) support us flagging with others when we are struggling?

You may want to use this exercise to uncover any areas of difference within your leadership team. For example, there may be areas of divergence on what the leadership team should be focusing its energy on, and why. These differences can be very productive sources of insight and analysis, bringing together different viewpoints and building clarity on what you will prioritize going forward.

Step 3: Enablers and inhibitors

As a third step, we suggest you next unpack the broad drivers of your performance on each of the Ps (or the specific elements within each of the Ps you identified in Step 2). What are the factors within your leadership team, and your wider organization, and outside the organization, that might explain your performance on each of the Ps? We suggest first identifying enablers. These are the factors that are helping you as a leadership team to get where you are on the bullseye or are driving your performance on Ps that you are doing relatively well on. Then, you want to do the reverse and identify inhibitors to your leadership team hitting the bullseye on each of the Ps.

Enablers and inhibitors could be more external to the team (e.g. industry trends, company policies or commitments made by the CEO) or more internal (e.g. how we are working together, how well we are living by and communicating our values, what kinds of strategic conversations we are having as a leadership team, how well we are prioritizing what we focus on, and what we directed our teams to focus on). As you do this exercise, consider how many of the enablers and inhibitors you have identified sit within your direct control, and how many are external and much less within your control. Are you being overly self-critical here and underplaying external drivers you cannot control? Or are you papering over drivers that are a product of your team's leadership to make yourselves appear more effective than you perhaps are? Typically, we would challenge leadership teams to identify one key enabler and one key inhibitor for each P. This forces you to make some decisions about what factors are really driving your leadership capability as a team and where you need to focus your attention.

From there, you should have four Ps, each with one enabler and one inhibitor. That's up to eight drivers of your leadership capability as a team. Now you might ask yourself: 'If we had to boil it down to its essence, what are the *three or four most important* drivers or inhibitors of our current performance as a leadership team, across the four Ps? What are the three or four most important factors that will be the difference between us hitting the bullseye on each of the Ps (or the Ps that we think are most important for us as an organization), and maintaining the status quo?'

This is a great opportunity to have an open conversation as to where you sit as a leadership group against the organization's goals and objectives, as well as in relation to those you lead (i.e. your staff and other key stakeholders). How aligned and unified are you as a leadership team about where you are at on these drivers? What are your points of difference? How can you build and achieve consensus on what your priorities are? When there are divisions within your leadership team on what your priorities ought to be, eliciting feedback from other stakeholders (e.g. staff members) can serve as a helpful circuit breaker by providing a third (and probably more impartial) view of the leadership team's performance.

However, when staff feedback is not possible, or such feedback fails to resolve differences of opinion among the leadership group, this is generally an important sign of deeper issues within the leadership team that need to be skilfully navigated. Mostly, teams tend to paper over points of difference, in the interests of 'moving on'. These points of divergence, however, represent an opportunity to uncover deeper attitudes, frustrations, agendas and viewpoints within the leadership team that, if not addressed, are sure to resurface in other, unhelpful ways. You can use these points of divergence within your team to unpack individuals' (or coalitions') different needs, perspectives, or agendas, in the interests of building clarity and alignment within your team. These kinds of conversations can be difficult to have, but if done respectfully and professionally, they serve to build clarity and alignment within the leadership group — both of which are precious commodities indeed!

Step 4: Actions

As a final step, summarize the key priorities for action under each of the three or four enablers/inhibitors identified above. What actions are needed to reinforce areas of strength? What actions are needed to turn around areas where you are not performing so well? You can again break into small groups to map out the actions that need to be taken under each of the Ps. As a part of this, consider whether there are similar actions on the list that might be consolidated, and which may be redundant based on existing, similar initiatives within the business or be rolled into these. At the end of the exercise there should be a clear, concrete set of actions that you as a leadership team will take to advance each of the Ps. Decide who within your leadership team will lead each initiative and allocate timeframes. Finally, you want to decide how regularly, and in what kind of way (e.g. an offsite), you wish to revisit these issues and assess your team's progress on its leadership capabilities.

Your personal leadership attributes

As a second reflective process, we now offer guidance on how you as an *individual* leader can achieve clarity on where your own strengths and weaknesses lie, against the four leadership attributes we share in this book. As we have articulated, we see these four attributes — authenticity, awareness, openness and balance — as crucial 'building blocks' of any leader sustaining themselves in an information-dense and hyper-connected working environment. To help you make progress on this, we now offer a set of reflective questions that you can consider and make notes in response to. Our advice is to start with your own assessment of how you are embodying these attributes as a leader. This kind of introspection enables you to step back and get a helicopter view of how you approach your leadership role, and how it impacts others. Your ambitions, aspirations, fears, beliefs and needs are best known to you, so we'd recommend starting with self-reflection. We advise making some notes in response to the questions under each of the four attributes. We typically suggest trying to fit your responses into a single A4 sheet of paper (or equivalent size if doing the exercise on a device) to keep answers concise. In responding to these questions, we suggest thinking across the broad gamut of your leadership role, rather than specific projects or key stakeholders.

Authenticity

» What are my three or four key values as a leader and my three or four key personal values?

» How well aligned are my leadership and personal values?

» How well am I living my values in my leadership role?

» How open am I in communicating my values and what is important to me?

» To what extent do I do what I say I will do (and not sign up to things I know I cannot do)?

Awareness

» To what extent am I able to compartmentalize my attention so I am focusing fully on the issue at hand?

» When would it make sense for me to include regular full-stops and commas in my day? How will I remind myself to implement these?

» How effective am I at unplugging from technology, especially after hours? How will I do this more effectively?

Openness

» How effectively do I engage with my most important relationships with an open attitude, listening to not only what they say, but also to the tone and intent behind their message?

» How well do I speak openly for the good of the whole, asking questions and challenging assumptions in a constructive but clear way?

» How effective am I at responding to threatening or stressful situations, rather than reacting impulsively?

» In relation to my key stakeholders, what balance do I strike between device-mediated communication and more direct, in-person communication? Do I have the balance right?

» What, if any, changes do I need to make in the communication modes I use with my key stakeholders?

Balance

» What are my three or four core priorities (i.e. rocks, pebbles, sand and water) and how effectively am I currently prioritizing these?

» Are there things I need to do to give these more energy and attention?

» Considering my professional and personal life, what level of functional reserve do I currently have for each of these?

» Are there changes I need to make to bolster these reserves?

» What daily, weekly, monthly and annual activities are core to me being able to self-renew regularly?

» How successful am I at engaging in these self-renewal activities? What changes do I need to make?

Having made some written notes in response to these questions, you can now step back and consider your responses as a whole. Are there any issues you obviously need to give greater attention and energy to? What are the actions that you can take that will help move you forward? Set yourself three or four actions to bring these capabilities to life for yourself. Make these actions SMART (specific, measurable, achievable, realistic and time-bound). As a leader, you want to be regularly visiting and revisiting these four leadership qualities, and how you are tracking with them. In the Appendices, we provide companion worksheets that can be used for this exercise.

Another step we would highly recommend is to elicit feedback from those you lead, or other key stakeholders who see your leadership on a daily basis. To what extent do your colleagues see you as embodying the four attributes? What do they see as your blind spots? You can send three or four colleagues these questions and let them anonymously provide brief written responses on each, in terms of how they perceive you. In the

Appendices we provide a set of brief reflection questions you can send your colleagues for feedback.

As a final step, you might want to take our questions and your responses to a trusted colleague, mentor, manager or leadership coach. Having a sounding board like this can help you test the feedback you have provided yourself (and any feedback your colleagues have provided). It can help clarify what the issues are, what is driving your strengths and limitations, and clarify your action points for the next six to twelve months.

Summary

In this chapter, we have provided suggested methods for engaging with the content of this book, both with your own senior leadership team, and for yourself, as a leader. Together, they provide two distinct, but equally valuable 'lenses' for you to audit your leadership performance and priorities for attention. Although the terrain and kinds of challenges contemporary leaders face are changing quite rapidly, we see the exercises in this chapter as foundational for sustained success — and, in many ways, timeless. In the next and final chapter, we lay out some of the issues we see as sitting on or just over the horizon, and that are likely to impact leaders' capacity to lead well over the coming years.

Chapter 7

Looking over the horizon

In one of the ancient Greek tales, Perseus, the son of Zeus, is tricked into agreeing to slay Medusa, a powerful and feared character whose gaze turns anyone who looks at her into stone.[1] Perseus is well aware of the danger Medusa poses, so acquires several aids to help him with his task: winged sandals (which enable him to fly), the cap of Hades (which confers invisibility), a curved sword to decapitate Medusa, and a bag in which to conceal Medusa's head. Lastly, Athena, the goddess of wisdom, gives Perseus a shield with a mirror, to use to guide himself to Medusa without ever looking at her directly (which would turn him into stone). Perseus uses the aids he has received to reach and slay Medusa.

Leaving aside the bloody details of the story, the aids Perseus received are like the various tools we've introduced in this book.

Although he is a highly skilled and competent warrior, Perseus needs additional tools and even 'special powers' to complete his task. He cannot do it alone, nor can he do it with only his raw talent. The tools serve as protections against Medusa's power. Our modern-day Medusa is information overwhelm and hyperactivity. In a similar way, the tools we have discussed in this book are the leader's aids. They are the 'inner tools' leaders need to cultivate to respond to the challenges of our time. But unlike Perseus' aids, which were specific to his task, the tools we offer are general and relevant across a wide arc of leadership situations where information overload impacts a leader's work.

We have outlined what we see as the key challenges for leaders in an environment of information overload. Whether it is communicating purpose, thinking clearly and prioritizing well, leading people or sustaining ourselves, the always-on work environment impacts all of these core leadership tasks. The key question is: How can leaders manage their work environment and deploy their attention so the result is clarity and effectiveness rather than overwhelm and confusion? In the preceding chapters we have proposed focus domains to consider — the four Ps — and practical methods and tools for leaders to experiment with. We now look ahead to consider some of the trends that we see impacting leaders' capacity to act with clarity in the years and decades to come.

Future challenges

Here we outline several broad trends that leaders will need to navigate in the years ahead. Some of these challenges are extensions of the challenges we have unpacked in previous chapters. Others are new and unprecedented shifts, the scope and reach of which we cannot fully foresee, but that will likely change what it means to lead well in the future. The common thread, though, is that each of these megatrends generates new ways in which information overload will impact leaders.

Hybrid is here to stay

For large slices of the population in most countries, the COVID-19 pandemic has fundamentally reset expectations about how and where work gets done. We do not see this reset being reverted quickly, especially in professions and industries where remote and/ or hybrid work can be done without compromising productivity. If anything, we see that hybrid work is here to stay. Companies such as Airbnb, Reddit, Dropbox and Atlassian, as well as global giants such as SAP, Fujitsu and Meta, have all committed publicly to permanent remote work options for staff. We see this trend continuing to snowball beyond the tech sector and into other service sectors such as banking and finance, accounting, design, legal and engineering. As the world's cities only get larger, there are big productivity gains to be had from hybrid work arrangements. This includes reduced commute times and costs, as well as wellbeing gains for employees. Hybrid work also allows companies to on-board talent from a larger, more geographically distributed pool than would have been previously considered. For some companies in sectors where talent is in high demand (e.g. data analytics and programming), offering highly flexible, remote work arrangements will remain a point of difference that companies will try to use to attract the best talent. In fact, not offering such arrangements will likely be a negative for current or prospective employees, leading to a loss of talent. Leaders will therefore need to develop and display skills in engaging and sustaining hybrid and remote employees' commitment and sense of connection to their colleagues and their organization.

The polarizing workplace

Another trend we see is increasing polarization, driven (partly at least) by the online world. For all its wonders, the internet has facilitated ever more rigid echo chambers that mean people right across the globe are increasingly polarized based on social, political and religious views. The stronger the identification with an in-group, the greater the potential for conflict with an out-group. Strong beliefs and opinions are constantly reinforced and strengthened, with the big tech algorithms (and in some cases, government policies) designed to feed people information that makes them feel more justified and wedded to their opinions (and more outraged against the counterview). As a result, we are more likely to keep consuming (and paying for) the narrative we already believe, and are less likely to be able to hear, let alone tolerate, different opinions.

All of this plays out in the workplace. Whether it manifests as rigidly held political views or, in global teams, as polarized cultural and political values, people's dependence on social media for information is only going to further amplify these trends. The core challenge, then, for leaders, is to create an environment where people can respectfully share their views and perspectives on issues that matter to them, while being willing and open to listening to different perspectives. A similar task applies for leading cross-cultural teams or teams with individuals from very different political systems (e.g. the US and China). The task for these leaders is to challenge themselves and their teams to listen, reach across the divide to be able to at least appreciate and understand the perspective of others, even if they don't agree with it, and to connect with a common humanity that unites rather than divides. The skills we discussed under People in Chapter 4 — an attitude of openness and inter-personal honesty, plus the capacity to listen fully and speak for the common good — are central to this. In particular, mindfulness-based practices have been shown to reduce in-group bias and polarization and help people to have higher regard for others, even those that would otherwise be in the out-group. [2,3]

Leading in an addicted world

As we have previously outlined, the power and impact of the online world is only just beginning to be felt. Humanity is collectively conducting one of the largest experiments the world has ever seen, and the macro-effects of this are only in their infancy. So-called 'digital natives' (e.g. people born around the advent of the iPhone in 2007) are teenagers. Looking ahead, we see technology playing an ever-greater role in our lives. Despite some efforts to pare back technology dependence by simplifying our tech lives and 'digital detoxing', the tide is overwhelmingly running the other way.[4,5] Based on the evidence to date, big tech is absolutely winning the battle for our attention.

In the workplace, we see the effects of this as only amplifying over the years ahead. As people's attentional capacities continue to be degraded, this will play out in employees' capacity to maintain focus, finish tasks, think strategically and make good decisions. Perhaps most of all, we see a huge challenge around employees' emotional resilience and capacity to manage stress. The hyper-connected and hyper-comparative world that social media has built, in turn spills over into a vulnerable and contingent sense of self-esteem and a loss of inner confidence and resilience.

This has huge implications for leaders trying to both embrace the online world of business and work, but also sustain the engagement and performance of people who are highly dependent on the online world — both attentionally and emotionally — and vulnerable to its impacts. Over the next decade, leaders will need to manage these vulnerabilities by being both sensitive to the realities of many employees' experiences, but also needing to provide support and resources to help staff manage their own mental health and capacity to be resilient. In all of this, leaders will need to be able to support themselves and sustain their own balance and mental wellbeing. Some of the tools and capacities we outline in this book, especially in Chapters 3 and 4, will be crucial for doing this.

The AI question

Perhaps the largest and most uncertain trend in the future of leadership is artificial intelligence. It is a technology with incredible potential, but even AI creators like Sam Altman warn about the potential ethical, legal and social dangers and the need for regulation.[6] With generative AI chatbots, for example, there is significant risk for bias, discrimination and manipulation of information based on the algorithms they are programmed with.[7]

AI is already changing the way many jobs get done. Whether it's using AI to respond to customer queries and complaints, to complete end-to-end manufacturing processes, to supplant wait staff in restaurants, to write essays or reports or to coach employees, AI is rapidly entering almost every sphere of human activity. Some experts point out that AI to date has been largely deployed for solving data-processing tasks that apply to a very specific and narrow function, such as in manufacturing and logistics. This is known as 'narrow AI'. In contrast, more complex 'generalized' AI, such as making judgement calls, replacing consultations with doctors and replacing normal social interaction, are finding their way into everyday life.[8] The question is, how far will the technology go, or be allowed to go? Initially, AI has largely taken more mundane work tasks from humans, rather than replacing human work roles entirely.[9] This has been described as 'taking the robot out of the human', rather than replacing the human altogether. However, even this is a massive challenge for employees and leaders in many industries. What is the impact of working with and through AI applications on employees' job satisfaction, work motivation and problem-solving capacities? What human needs are robots unable to meet? For example, what do leaders need to do to ensure organizational culture, trust, proactivity and innovation do not suffer as a result of the apparent gains from greater AI in the workplace? The answers to these questions will doubtless vary greatly with the kind of automation, industry and job type that is affected. But either way, these changes are likely to have big impacts on the world of work and the role of leaders in managing staff.

Perhaps a bigger question is what happens when AI moves from narrow to general AI? That is, when AI begins to replicate the more sophisticated, general intelligence capacities that to date are the preserve of homo sapiens. What will happen as humans are less and less able to distinguish between 'reality' based on evidence and an 'alternate reality' generated by AI and less based on evidence? Experts point to the idea of a 'j-curve' with AI development following the path of much technology development of the past: there is a three- to four-decade period of (largely unnoticed) development, before an explosion in uptake across businesses and societies.[10] Think aeroplane flight, driving, personal computing, the internet and the smartphone. Arguably, we are already at this tipping point.

As humanity approaches more general AI, this will raise massive questions for leadership. Might AI be able to displace leaders altogether? What happens if/when it does? What is it that humans can bring to the table that a machine, albeit a very intelligent one, can't? That case will increasingly need to be made. The intelligence and processing capacity of cutting-edge robots may mean they are deployed to help plan work priorities, allocate work tasks across teams, monitor project performance and solve business problems. If it becomes ubiquitous, will humans become mentally lazy, complacent and inattentive? Could the leader even become redundant? We do not think so, given the deeply human work of great leadership and inspiration, as we have outlined. However, the rise and rise of AI places these questions front and centre of the future of leadership — with perhaps a narrowing of leaders' work, to focus on more human-centred and strategic issues.

These are big questions and, perhaps because of the 'j-curve' manner in which these technologies tend to develop, it is difficult to precisely predict the various ways in which AI will impact leaders and the organizations they run. We are collectively running an experiment unprecedented in human history. The results are already starting to pour in. The question is, will we have the will, wit and awareness to read and understand them and then to calibrate the way we use AI?

The virtual world

The last of the future challenges we will explore here relates to living and working in the world of virtual reality (VR). Like any (relatively) new technology, the premature promise of great benefits and the unbridled enthusiasm are prominent but the actual effects and uses of 'real world' VR are still largely untested. On the positive side, there is some evidence to support the use of VR in reducing stress and inducing relaxation in the workplace, as it has been demonstrated to do in healthcare settings.[11,12] There are also emerging possible uses such as skills training or being able to virtually design and test office or industrial workplaces, production lines and procedures using VR.[13,14, 15,16] On the negative side, one review of the literature pointed to potential downsides such as inducing 'cybersickness symptoms' that may prevent workers from using VR.[17] Such symptoms include more visual fatigue, muscle fatigue and musculoskeletal discomfort, higher stress (due to technostress, task difficulty, time pressure and public speaking) and mental overload (due to task load, time pressure and the virtual environment interface). Perhaps of even greater concern is that even after one episode of VR use, a significant number of people experience symptoms of depersonalization and derealization (blurring of the sense of reality).[18,19] These are concerning outcomes for the individual but may have even greater implications for teams. Further, it is estimated that between 2 per cent and 20 per cent of users reveal compulsive VR use, although this is similar to other more traditional technologies.[20] This level of addiction may prove to be an underestimate, however, as VR becomes more ubiquitous and the technology becomes more sophisticated and realistic.

What the long-term impacts are for how VR influences how people collaborate or communicate is hardly known, but as with any new or emerging technology, the enthusiasm and marketing hype can run well ahead of what it can actually deliver, and the potential harms tend to be downplayed. In the future it may be best to only adopt specific uses of VR in the workplace once the benefits for that use have been established and the harms have been well defined and mitigated.

Final thoughts

As we have articulated in this book, we see a core set of leadership capabilities as fundamental for leaders in an information-dense world, and also for navigating the future trends we've just discussed. Based on the research to date and our own experience, we have identified four core leadership domains (i.e. the four Ps) that we see being threatened by information overwhelm. The four Ps (Purpose, Priorities, People and Personal) are critical issues leaders need to handle well in order to survive. The future demands on leaders are likely to become more complex and varied, pulling leaders' attention ever more 'out there', to the immediate, fleeting and often superficial issues of the moment.

It is precisely *because* of this increasing complexity, change and sheer volume of information, that we see the foundational priorities and attributes we point to in this book as being increasingly vital for any leader to be able to function well. Whether you are building a new business, leading a large corporation or directing a public agency, you are inevitably grappling with how to best deploy your attention. Rather than acquiring ever more technical skill, or jumping on new fads and 'silver bullets', we see the core 'inner work' of leaders as being the difference between future success and failure. For each of the four Ps, we have offered a series of mini experiments and reflection questions to help you as a leader navigate these challenges and sharpen the capacities of your leadership team.

As well as this, within each of the four Ps, we have proposed four 'inner' leadership attributes (authenticity, awareness, openness and balance) that we see as being pivotal for any leaders' success in the information age. These attributes are by no means new, but are now more needed than perhaps ever before, as the tidal wave of information competes for our attention and our energy. The extent to which we, as leaders, can hold on to, and strengthen, these four personal attributes will in large part determine our leadership success in the age of info-whelm. A bit like a rocky island in the middle of a huge, fast-flowing river, these four attributes can be a crucial vantage point that we can clamber onto and from which we can gain clarity on how we should move ahead. With these attributes, we can decide wisely, respond consciously and, for those who depend on us, lead with clarity.

Appendices

Template 1: Leadership team bullseye

We are clear on the needs we exist to serve, and the values that deliver this. Our purpose is clearly reflected in the decisions we take as a leadership team and is well integrated across our team/organization.

We are consistently focused on the right strategic issues. We are good at stepping back and seeing the bigger picture, but can also 'seize the moment' when we need to move fast. As a leadership team, we engage with each other with full attention, non-reactivity and honesty.

Purpose: _____

Priorities: _____

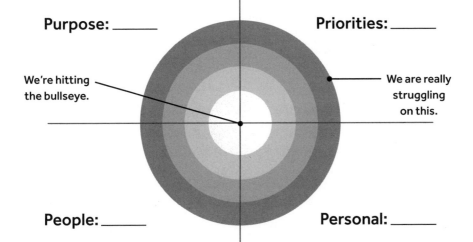

We're hitting the bullseye.

We are really struggling on this.

People: _____

Personal: _____

As a leadership team, we embody qualities of openness, interpersonal honesty and presence when we engage with each other and those we lead.

As a leadership team, we have the appropriate amount of 'functional reserve'. We look after our own wellbeing and resilience, so that we can sustain ourselves in our leadership role. We look out for each other. We role model self-care among those we lead.

Template 2: Leadership self-reflection

Leadership attribute 1: Authenticity

Below is a set of reflection questions that you, as a leader, can consider in relation to the attribute of authenticity. You can jot your answers down on a separate piece of paper.

» What are my three or four key values as a leader? What are my three or four key personal values?

» How well aligned are my leadership and personal values?

» How well, on a scale of 1 to10, am I living my values in my leadership role? (Think of examples where you have recently acted in a values-aligned way? What about examples where you have not? Which scenario is more common for you?)

» How open am I in communicating my values and what is important to me? What supports me in communicating my values, and what gets in the way of this?

» To what extent do I do what I say I will do (and not sign up to things I know I cannot do)?

Discuss your responses to the above questions with a mentor, trusted colleague or coach. What common threads or insights emerge?

Actions: Based on the above reflection, what two to three actions will help strengthen authenticity in myself as a leader? You might like to draw up your own table and complete it on a separate piece of paper.

Action description	Why does this action matter to me?	Specific steps / 'sub-actions'	Timeframes for completing each step

Leadership attribute 2: Awareness

Below is a set of reflection questions that you, as a leader, can consider in relation to the attribute of awareness.

» To what extent am I able to 'compartmentalize' my attention so I am focusing fully on the issue at hand? What habits/ practices would help me to do this more consistently?

» When would make sense for me to include regular 'full stops' and 'commas' in my day? How will I remind myself to implement these?

» How effective am I at unplugging from technology, especially after hours? How will I do this more effectively?

Discuss your responses to the above questions with a mentor, trusted colleague or coach. What common threads or insights emerge?

Actions: Based on the above reflection, what two to three actions will help strengthen awareness in myself as a leader?

Action description	Why does this action matter to me?	Specific steps / 'sub-actions'	Timeframes for completing each step

Leadership attribute 3: Openness

Below is a set of reflection questions that you, as a leader, can consider in relation to the attribute of openness.

- » How effectively do I engage with my most important relationships with an open attitude, listening to what they say, as well as the tone and intent behind their message? What are my priorities for listening well?
- » How well do I speak openly for the good of the whole, asking questions and challenging assumptions in a constructive but clear way? What do I need to work on for this capability?
- » How effective am I at responding to threatening or stressful situations, rather than reacting impulsively? What do I need to work on for this capability?
- » In relation to my key stakeholders, what balance do I strike between device-mediated communication and more direct, in-person communication? Do I have the balance right?
- » What, if any, changes do I need to make in the communication modes I use with my key stakeholders?

Discuss your responses to the above questions with a mentor, trusted colleague or coach. What common threads or insights emerge?

Actions: Based on the above reflection, what two to three actions will help strengthen openness in myself as a leader?

Action description	Why does this action matter to me?	Specific steps / 'sub-actions'	Timeframes for completing each step

Leadership attribute 4: Balance

Below is a set of reflection questions that you, as a leader, can consider in relation to the attribute of balance.

» What are my three or four core priorities (i.e. rocks, versus pebbles, sand and water) and how effectively am I currently prioritizing my core priorities?

» Are there things I need to do to give my rocks more energy and attention?

» Considering my professional and personal life, what level of functional reserve do I currently have for each of these? Are there changes I need to make to bolster these reserves?

» What daily, weekly, monthly and annual activities are core to me being able to self-renew regularly?

» How successful am I at engaging in these self-renewal activities? What changes do I need to make?

Discuss your responses to the above questions with a mentor, trusted colleague or coach. What common threads or insights emerge?

Actions: Based on the above reflection, what two to three actions will help strengthen balance in myself as a leader?

Action description	Why does this action matter to me?	Specific steps / 'sub-actions'	Timeframes for completing each step

Template 3: Reflection questions for colleagues

Below are several open-ended questions for you to respond to in relation to your colleague [insert name here]. Please answer these as directly as you can.

Authenticity

» Based on what you see and know about your colleague, what are their three or four key values as a leader?
» How well is your colleague living their values in their leadership role?
» How open is your colleague in communicating their values and what is important to them?
» To what extent do they do what they say they will do?

Awareness

» To what extent is your colleague able to 'compartmentalize' their attention, so they are focusing fully on the issue at hand?
» How good is your colleague at being in the moment and attending to one task or conversation at a time?

Openness

» How well does your colleague speak openly for the good of the whole, asking questions, and challenging assumptions in a constructive but clear way?

» How effective is your colleague at responding to threatening or stressful situations, rather than reacting impulsively?

» What balance does your colleague strike between device-mediated communication and more direct, in-person communication?

» What changes, if any, does your colleague need to make in the communication modes they use with key stakeholders?

Balance

» As far as you can tell, what level of functional reserve does your colleague currently have?

» As far as you can tell, how successful is your colleague at engaging in self-renewal activities?

References

Introduction

1. The names of individuals in the personal anecdotes we refer to in this book are pseudonyms.
2. Stoker, J. I., Garretsen, H., & Lammers, J. (2022). 'Leading and working from home in times of COVID-19: On the perceived changes in leadership behaviours.' *Journal of Leadership & Organizational Studies, 29*(2), 208–218.
3. Firth, J., Torous, J., Stubbs, B., Firth, J. A., Steiner, G. Z., Smith, L., ... & Sarris, J. (2019). 'The "online brain": How the Internet may be changing our cognition.' *World Psychiatry, 18*(2), 119–129.

Chapter 1

1. Kelly, G. (2017). *Live, Lead, Learn: My stories of life and leadership.* Penguin Group Australia; unpublished remarks provided by Gail Kelly in a 2011 speech at Commonwealth Treasury, Canberra Australia.
2. Garvin, D. A., & Roberto, M. A. (2001). 'What you don't know about making decisions.' *Harvard Business Review, 79*(8), 108–119.
3. Hallowell, E. M. (2005). 'Overloaded circuits: Why smart people

underperform.' *Harvard Business Review, 83*(1), 54–116.

4.   Mark, G., Iqbal, S., Czerwinski, M., & Johns, P. (2015, February). 'Focused, aroused, but so distractible: Temporal perspectives on multitasking and communications.' In *Proceedings of the 18th ACM Conference on Computer Supported Cooperative Work & Social Computing* (pp. 903–916).

5.   Chong, J., & Siino, R. (2006, November). 'Interruptions on software teams: A comparison of paired and solo programmers.' In *Proceedings of the 2006 20th Anniversary Conference on Computer Supported Cooperative Work* (pp. 29–38).

6.   Bernstein, E., & Waber, B. (2019). 'The truth about open offices.' *Harvard Business Review, 97*(6), 83.

7.   Molla, R. (2019, May 1). 'The productivity pit: How Slack is ruining work.' https://www.vox.com/recode/2019/5/1/18511575/productivity-slack–google–microsoft–facebook

8.   Wajcman, J., & Rose, E. (2011). 'Constant connectivity: Rethinking interruptions at work.' *Organization Studies, 32*(7), 941–961.

9.   Perlow, L. A. (1999). 'The time famine: Toward a sociology of work time.' *Administrative Science Quarterly,* 44, 57–81

10. Perlow, L., & Weeks, J. (2002). 'Who's helping whom? Layers of culture and workplace behavior.' *Journal of Organizational Behavior, 23,* 345–361.

11. Mazmanian, M., Orlikowski, W. J., & Yates, J. (2013). 'The autonomy paradox: The implications of mobile email devices for knowledge professionals.' *Organization Science,* 24(5), 1337–1357.

12. Mattarelli, E., Bertolotti, F., & Incerti, V. (2015). 'The interplay between organizational polychronicity, multitasking behaviors and organizational identification: A mixed-methods study in knowledge intensive organizations.' *International Journal of Human–Computer Studies, 79,* 6–19.

13. Alliance. (2013). 'Survey for white-collar worker mobile phone use.' http://article.zhaopin.com/pub/print.jsp?id¼212276

14. Lee, K. H., & Kim, K. S. (2015). A study on the impact of the use of smart devices on work and life. https://www.kli.re.kr/kli/rsrchReprtView.do?pblctListNo¼8663&key¼13.

15. Park, J. C., Kim, S., & Lee, H. (2020). 'Effect of work-related smartphone use after work on job burnout: Moderating effect of social support and organizational politics.' *Computers in Human Behavior, 105,* 106194.

16. Ophir, E., Nass, C., & Wagner, A. D. (2009). 'Cognitive control in media multitaskers.' *Proc. Natl. Acad. Sci. U.S.A. 106,* 15583–15587. doi:

10.1073/pnas.0903620106

17. Gajendran, R. S., Loewenstein, J., Choi, H., & Ozgen, S. (2022). 'Hidden costs of text-based electronic communication on complex reasoning tasks: Motivation maintenance and impaired downstream performance.' *Organizational Behavior and Human Decision Processes*, *169*, 104130.

18. Clinton-Lisell, V. (2021). 'Stop multitasking and just read: Meta-analyses of multitasking's effects on reading performance and reading time.' *Journal of Research in Reading*, *44*(4), 787–816. https://doi.org/10.1111/1467–9817.12372

19. Sanbonmatsu, D. M., Strayer, D. L., Medeiros-Ward, N., & Watson, J. M. (2013). 'Who multi-tasks and why? Multi-tasking ability, perceived multitasking ability, impulsivity, and sensation seeking.' *PLoS ONE*, 8, e54402. doi: 10.1371/journal.pone.0054402

20. Wilmer, H. H., & Chein, J. M. (2016). 'Mobile technology habits: Patterns of association among device usage, intertemporal preference, impulse control, and reward sensitivity.' *Psychon. Bull. Rev.*, *23*, 1607–1614. doi: 10.3758/s13423–016–1011–z

21. Ciarrochi, J., Parker, P., Sahdra, B., Marshall, S., Jackson, C., Gloster, A. T., & Heaven, P. (2016). 'The development of compulsive internet use and mental health: A four-year study of adolescence.' *Developmental Psychology*, *52*(2), 272.

22. Donald, J. N., Ciarrochi, J., Parker, P. D., & Sahdra, B. K. (2019). 'Compulsive internet use and the development of self-esteem and hope: A four-year longitudinal study.' *Journal of Personality*, *87*(5), 981–995.

23. Donald, J. N., Ciarrochi, J., & Sahdra, B. K. (2022). 'The consequences of compulsion: A 4-year longitudinal study of compulsive internet use and emotion regulation difficulties.' *Emotion*, *22*(4), 678.

Chapter 2

1. Useem, M. (2018). https://knowledge.wharton.upenn.edu/podcast/knowledge-at-wharton-podcast/leadership-lessons-thai-soccer-team-rescue/ 2018.

2. Ryan, R. M., & Deci, E. L. (2017). *Self-determination theory: Basic psychological needs in motivation, development, and wellness.* Guilford Publications.

3.   Di Domenico, S. I., & Ryan, R. M. (2017). 'The emerging neuroscience of intrinsic motivation: A new frontier in self-determination research.' *Frontiers in Human Neuroscience*, 11, 145.

4.   Ashby, F. G., Isen, A. M., & Turken, A. U. (1999). 'A neuropsychological theory of positive affect and its influence on cognition.' *Psychol. Rev. 106*, 529–550. doi: 10.1037/0033–295x.106.3.529

5.   Salamone, J. D., & Correa, M. (2016). 'Neurobiology of effort and the role of mesolimbic dopamine.' In *Advances in Motivation and Achievement: Recent developments in neuroscience research on human motivation*, eds S. Kim, J. Reeve & M. Bong. Emerald Group Publishing, 229–256.

6.   Di Domenico, S. I., & Ryan, R. M. (2017). 'The emerging neuroscience of intrinsic motivation: A new frontier in self-determination research.' *Frontiers in human neuroscience, 11*, 145.

7.   Ulrich, M., Keller, J., Hoenig, K., Waller, C., & Grön, G. (2014). 'Neural correlates of experimentally induced flow experiences.' *Neuroimage, 86*, 194–202. doi: 10.1016/j.neuroimage.2013.08.019

8.   Sperling, R. A., LaViolette, P. S., O'Keefe, K., O'Brien, J., Rentz, D. M., Pihlajamaki, M., ... & Johnson, K. A. (2009). 'Amyloid deposition is associated with impaired default network function in older persons without dementia'. *Neuron, 63*(2), 178–188.

9.   Boyer-Davis, S. (2018). 'The relationship between technology stress and leadership style: An empirical investigation.' *Journal of Business and Educational Leadership, 8*(1), 48–65.

10. Starcke, K., Pawlikowski, M., Wolf, O. T., Altstötter-Gleich, C., & Brand, M. (2011). 'Decision-making under risk conditions is susceptible to interference by a secondary executive task.' *Cognitive Processing, 12*(2), 177–182. https://doi.org/10.1007/s10339–010–0387–3

11. Baror, S., & Bar, M. (2016). 'Associative activation and its relation to exploration and exploitation in the brain.' *Psychological Science, 27*(6), 776–789. https://doi.org/10.1177/0956797616634487

12. Scafuri Kovalchuk, L., Buono, C., Ingusci, E., Maiorano, F., De Carlo, E., Madaro, A., & Spagnoli, P. (2019). 'Can work engagement be a resource for reducing workaholism's undesirable outcomes? A multiple mediating model including moderated mediation analysis.' *International Journal of Environmental research and Public Health, 16*(8), 1402. https://doi.org/10.3390/ijerph16081402

13. Janssen, M., Heerkens, Y., Kuijer, W., van der Heijden, B., & Engels, J.

(2018). 'Effects of mindfulness-based stress reduction on employees' mental health: A systematic review.' *PloS one*, *13*(1), e0191332. https://doi.org/10.1371/journal.pone.0191332

14. Prudenzi, A., Graham, C. D., Clancy, F., Hill, D., O'Driscoll, R., Day, F., & O'Connor, D. B. (2021). 'Group-based acceptance and commitment therapy interventions for improving general distress and work-related distress in healthcare professionals: A systematic review and meta-analysis.' *Journal of Affective Disorders*, *295*, 192–202.

15. Kitayama, S., Akutsu, S., Uchida, Y., & Cole, S. W. (2016). 'Work, meaning, and gene regulation: Findings from a Japanese information technology firm.' *Psychoneuroendocrinology*, *72*, 175–181. https://doi.org/10.1016/j.psyneuen.2016.07.004

16. Edgar Schein's famous research on workplace culture finds that organisational culture is shaped by the 'underlying assumptions' that sit beneath the surface in any organisation (i.e. are not visible), but that shape the values and behaviours within that organisation. In seeking to shift the culture, Schein suggests leaders ask themselves: 'What problems can we create that the organisation can adapt to solve?' By identifying a set of problems, the organisation will adapt to solve these, hence changing the culture with it. This approach has parallels to how we think of purpose and how to articulate it. Schein, E. H. (2010). *Organizational Culture and Leadership* (Vol. 2). John Wiley & Sons.

17. Çiçek, B., & Kılınç, E. (2021). 'Can transformational leadership eliminate the negativity of technostress? Insights from the logistic industry.' *Business & Management Studies: An International Journal, 9*(1), 372–384.

18. Starcke, K., Pawlikowski, M., Wolf, O. T., Altstötter-Gleich, C., & Brand, M. (2011). 'Decision-making under risk conditions is susceptible to interference by a secondary executive task.' *Cognitive Processing*, *12*(2), 177–182. https://doi.org/10.1007/s10339-010-0387-3

19. Beilock, S. L., & Carr, T. H. (2005). 'When high-powered people fail: Working memory and "choking under pressure" in math.' *Psychological Science*, *16*(2), 101–105. https://doi.org/10.1111/j.0956-7976.2005.00789.x

20. https://www.etymonline.com/word/authentic

21. Ziano, I., & Wang, D. (2021). 'Slow lies: Response delays promote perceptions of insincerity.' *Journal of Personality and Social Psychology, 120*(6), 1457–1479. https://doi.org/10.1037/pspa0000250.

22. Coutifaris, C. G., & Grant, A. M. (2022). 'Taking your team behind the curtain: The effects of leader feedback-sharing and feedback-seeking on team psychological safety.' *Organization Science*, *33*(4), 1574–1598.

Chapter 3

1. Covey, S., Merrill, R., & Merrill, R. R. (1996). *First Things First: To live, to love, to learn, to leave a legacy*. Simon and Schuster.
2. Moolman, T., & Mankins, M. (2017, March 1). 'Digital tools are helpful in increasing productivity.' https://www.bain.com/insights/digital–tools–are–helpful–in–increasing–productivity–businessday/ Originally appeared in *Business Day*, https://www.businesslive.co.za/bd/opinion/2017–03–01–digital–tools–are–helpful–in–increasing–productivity/
3. Molla, R. (2019, May 1). 'The productivity pit: How Slack is ruining work.' https://www.vox.com/recode/2019/5/1/18511575/productivity–slack–google–microsoft–facebook
4. Clifford, C. (2014, November 23). 'How much time do your employees spend doing real work?' *Entrepreneur*. https://www.entrepreneur.com/article/240076
5. Dillard-Wright, D. B. (2018). 'Technology designed for addiction.' *Psychology Today*. https://www.psychologytoday.com/au/blog/boundless/201801/technology–designed–addiction
6. https://www.realclearpolitics.com/video/2017/12/11/fmr_facebook_exec_social_media_is_ripping_our_social_fabric_apart.html
7. Hallowell, E. M. (2005). 'Overloaded circuits: Why smart people underperform.' *Harvard Business Review*, *83*(1), 54–116.
8. http://time.com/3858309/attention–spans–goldfish/
9. Makary, M. A., & Daniel, M. (2016). 'Medical error – the third leading cause of death in the US.' *BMJ (Clinical research ed.)*, *353*, i2139. https://doi.org/10.1136/bmj.i2139
10. Distracted Driving. (2022). Australian Automobile Association. https://www.aaa.asn.au/research/distracted–driving/
11. Stothart, C., Mitchum, A., & Yehnert, C. (2015). 'The attentional cost of receiving a cell phone notification.' *Journal of Experimental Psychology. Human Perception and Performance*, *41*(4), 893–897. https://doi.org/10.1037/xhp0000100
12. Ward, A. F., Duke, K., Gneezy, A., & Bos, M. W. (2017). 'Brain drain: The

mere presence of one's own smartphone reduces available cognitive capacity.' *JACR, 2*(2), 140–154. http://dx.doi.org/10.1086/691462

13. Baror, S., & Bar, M. (2016). 'Associative activation and its relation to exploration and exploitation in the brain.' *Psychological Science, 27*(6), 776–789. https://doi.org/10.1177/0956797616634487

14. Starcke, K., Pawlikowski, M., Wolf, O. T., Altstötter-Gleich, C., & Brand, M. (2011). 'Decision-making under risk conditions is susceptible to interference by a secondary executive task.' *Cognitive Processing, 12*(2), 177–182. https://doi.org/10.1007/s10339-010-0387-3

15. Hallowell, E. M. (2005). 'Overloaded circuits: Why smart people underperform.' *Harvard Business Review, 83*(1), 54–116.

16. Rumelt, R. (2022). *The Crux: How leaders become strategists.* Profile Books.

17. Firth, J., Torous, J., Stubbs, B., et al. (2019). 'The "online brain": How the Internet may be changing our cognition.' *World Psychiatry, 18*(2), 119–129. doi: 10.1002/wps.20617.

18. Interview conducted by Anderson Cooper with Amishi Jha and Major General Piatt. https://www.youtube.com/watch?v=pN64uJlRasI

19. Nassif, T., Adrian, A., Gutierrez, I., Dixon, A., Rogers, S., Jha, A., & Adler, A. (2021). 'Optimizing performance and mental skills with mindfulness-based attention training: Two field studies with operational units'. *Military Medicine.* 10.1093/milmed/usab380.

20. https://www.mindful.org/youre-overwhelmed-and-its-not-your-fault/

21. Davis, M. C., Leach, D. J., & Clegg, C. W. (2011). 'The physical environment of the office: Contemporary and emerging issues.' In *International Review of Industrial and Organizational Psychology* (Volume 26), eds G. P. Hodgkinson & J. K. Ford. Wiley Online Library. https://doi.org/10.1002/9781119992592.ch6

22. Rosling, H. (2018). *Factfulness: Ten reasons we're wrong about the world – and why things are better than you think.* Sceptre.

23. Gajendran, R. S., Loewenstein, J., Choi, H., & Ozgen, S. (2022). 'Hidden costs of text-based electronic communication on complex reasoning tasks: Motivation maintenance and impaired downstream performance.' *Organizational Behavior and Human Decision Processes, 169*, 104130.

24. Jackson, T., Dawson, R., & Wilson, D. (2001). 'The cost of email interruption.' *Journal of Systems and Information Technology, 5*(1), 81–92. https://doi.org/10.1108/13287260180000760

25. Colzato, L. S., Ozturk, A., & Hommel, B. (2012). 'Meditate to create: The impact of focused-attention and open-monitoring training on convergent and divergent thinking.' *Frontiers in Psychology*, *3*, 116. https://doi.org/10.3389/fpsyg.2012.00116

26. Atkins, P. W. B., Hassed, C., & Fogliati, V. J. (2015). 'Mindfulness improves work engagement, wellbeing and performance in a university setting.' In *Flourishing in Life, Work, and Careers*, eds R. J. Burke, C. L. Cooper & K. M. Page. Elgar, pp. 193–209.

27. Reb, J., Narayanan, J., & Chaturvedi, S. (2012). 'Leading mindfully: Two studies on the influence of supervisor trait mindfulness on employee wellbeing and performance.' *Mindfulness*, *1*(1). doi:10.1007/s12671–012–0144–z

28. Walsh, M. M., & Arnold, K. A. (2018). 'Mindfulness as a buffer of leaders' self-rated behavioral responses to emotional exhaustion: A dual process model of self-regulation.' *Front Psychol.*, *9*, 2498. doi: 10.3389/fpsyg.2018.02498.

29. Garland, E. L., Farb, N. A., Goldin, P. R., & Fredrickson, B. L. (2015). 'The mindfulness-to-meaning theory: Extensions, applications, and challenges at the attention–appraisal–emotion interface.' *Psychological Inquiry*, *26*(4), 377–387, DOI: 10.1080/1047840X.2015.1092493

30. Hjemdal, O., Solem, S., Hagen, R., Kennair, L., Nordahl, H. M., & Wells, A. (2019). 'A randomized controlled trial of metacognitive therapy for depression: Analysis of 1-year follow-up.' *Frontiers in Psychology*, *10*, 1842. https://doi.org/10.3389/fpsyg.2019.01842

31. Kruger, J., & Dunning, D. (1999). 'Unskilled and unaware of it: How difficulties in recognizing one's own incompetence lead to inflated self-assessments.' *Journal of Personality and Social Psychology*, *77*(6), 1121.

32. Garland, E. L., Hanley, A. W., Goldin, P. R., & Gross, J. J. (2017). 'Testing the mindfulness-to-meaning theory: Evidence for mindful positive emotion regulation from a reanalysis of longitudinal data.' *PloS one*, *12*(12), e0187727. https://doi.org/10.1371/journal.pone.0187727

33. Sibinga, E. M., & Wu, A. W. (2010). 'Clinician mindfulness and patient safety.' *JAMA*, *304*(22), 2532–3.

34. Hafenbrack, A. C., Kinias, Z., & Barsade, S. G. (2014). 'Debiasing the mind through meditation: Mindfulness and the sunk-cost bias.' *Psychological Science*, *25*(2), 369–376. https://doi.org/10.1177/0956797613503853

35. Ruedy, N. E., & Schweitzer, M. E. (2010). 'In the moment: The effect

of mindfulness on ethical decision making.' *J Bus Ethics, 95*(Suppl 1), 73–87. https://doi.org/10.1007/s10551-011-0796-y

36. Janssen, M., Heerkens, Y., Kuijer, W., van der Heijden, B., & Engels, J. (2018). 'Effects of mindfulness-based stress reduction on employees' mental health: A systematic review.' *PloS one, 13*(1), e0191332. https://doi.org/10.1371/journal.pone.0191332

37. Hülsheger, U. R., Alberts, H. J., Feinholdt, A., & Lang, J. W. (2013). 'Benefits of mindfulness at work: The role of mindfulness in emotion regulation, emotional exhaustion, and job satisfaction.' *Journal of Applied Psychology, 98*(2), 310–325. https://doi.org/10.1037/a0031313

38. Reb, J., Narayanan, J., & Chaturvedi, S. (2014). 'Leading mindfully: Two studies on the influence of supervisor trait mindfulness on employee well-being and performance.' *Mindfulness, 5*(1), 36–45 https://doi.org/10.1007/s12671-012-0144-z

39. Reb, J., Narayanan, J., & Ho, Z. W. (2015). 'Mindfulness at work: Antecedents and consequences of employee awareness and absent-mindedness.' *Mindfulness, 6*(1), 111–122. https://doi.org/10.1007/s12671-013-0236-4

40. Schultz, P. P., Ryan, R. M., Niemiec, C. P., et al. (2015). 'Mindfulness, work climate, and psychological need satisfaction in employee well-being.' *Mindfulness, 6*, 971–985. https://doi.org/10.1007/s12671-014-0338-7

41. Purser, R. (2019). *McMindfulness: How mindfulness became the new capitalist spirituality.* Penguin.

42. Hafenbrack, A. C., & Vohs, K. D. (2018). 'Mindfulness meditation impairs task motivation but not performance.' *Organizational Behavior and Human Decision Processes, 147*, 1–15. https://doi.org/10.1016/j.obhdp.2018.05.001

43. Marion-Jetten, A. S., Taylor, G., & Schattke, K. (2022). 'Mind your goals, mind your emotions: Mechanisms explaining the relation between dispositional mindfulness and action crises.' *Personality & Social Psychology Bulletin, 48*(1), 3–18. https://doi.org/10.1177/0146167220986310

44. Niemiec, C. P., Ryan, R. M., & Deci, E. L. (2009). 'The path taken: Consequences of attaining intrinsic and extrinsic aspirations in post-college life.' *J Res Pers., 73*(3), 291–306. doi: 10.1016/j.jrp.2008.09.001.

Chapter 4

1. Fifield, A. (2019, March 18). 'New Zealand's prime minister receives worldwide praise for her response to the mosque shootings.' *Washington Post.* https://www.washingtonpost.com/world/2019/03/18/new–zealands–prime–minister–wins–worldwide–praise–her–response–mosque–shootings/

2. https://www.npr.org/2010/01/18/122701268/i–have–a–dream–speech–in–its–entirety

3. https://www.nobelprize.org/prizes/peace/1979/teresa/biographical/

4. https://winstonchurchill.org/the–life–of–churchill/life/man–of–words/churchill–the–orator/

5. Zaleznik, A. (2004). 'Managers and leaders: Are they different?' *Harvard Business Review.* https://hbr.org/2004/01/managers–and–leaders–are–they–different

6. https://time.com/person–of–the–year–2022–volodymyr–zelensky/

7. Lowe, K. B., Kroeck, K. G., & Sivasubramaniam, N. (1996). 'Effectiveness correlates of transformational and transactional leadership: A meta-analytic review of the MLQ literature.' *Leadership Quarterly, 7*(3), 385–425.

8. Maslach, C., & Jackson, S.E. (1981). 'The measurement of experienced burnout.' *Journal of Organizational Behavior, 2*, 99–113. http://dx.doi.org/10.1002/job.4030020205

9. https://www.thoracic.org/patients/patient–resources/resources/burnout–syndrome.pdf

10. Holtgraves, T. (2022). 'Implicit communication of emotions via written text messages.' *Computers in Human Behavior Reports, 7.* https://doi.org/10.1016/j.chbr.2022.100219.

11. Beach, M. C., Roter, D., Korthuis, P. T., Epstein, R. M., et al. (2013). 'A multicenter study of physician mindfulness and health care quality.' *Ann Fam Med, 11*(5), 421–428. doi: 10.1370/afm.1507

12. Gajendran, R. S., Javalagi, A., Wang, C., & Ponnapalli, A. R. (2021). 'Consequences of remote work use and intensity: A meta-analysis.' *Academy of Management Proceedings, 1.* https://doi.org/10.5465/AMBPP.2021.15255abstract

13. Donald, J. N., Ciarrochi, J., Parker, P. D., & Sahdra, B. K. (2019). 'Compulsive internet use and the development of self-esteem and hope: A four-year longitudinal study.' *Journal of Personality, 87*(5), 981–995.

14. Firth, J., Torous, J., Stubbs, B., et al. (2019). 'The "online brain": How the Internet may be changing our cognition.' *World Psychiatry, 18*(2), 119–129.

15. Frith, C. D. (2008). 'Social cognition'. *Philos Trans R Soc Lond B Biol Sci, 363*(1499), 2033–9. doi: 10.1098/rstb.2008.0005.

16. Donald, J. N., Ciarrochi, J., & Sahdra, B. K. (2022). 'The consequences of compulsion: A 4-year longitudinal study of compulsive internet use and emotion regulation difficulties.' *Emotion, 22*(4), 678.

17. Donald, J. N., Ciarrochi, J., & Guo, J. (2022). 'Connected or cutoff? A 4-year longitudinal study of the links between adolescents' compulsive internet use and social support.' *Personality and Social Psychology Bulletin.* https://doi.org/10.1177/01461672221127802

18. Lapierre, M. A., & Zhao, P. (2022). 'Smartphones and social support: Longitudinal associations between smartphone use and types of support.' *Social Science Computer Review, 40*(3), 831–843.

19. Singer, T., & Klimecki, O. M. (2014). 'Empathy and compassion.' *Current Biology, 24*(18), R875–R878.

20. Klimecki, O., & Singer, T. (2012). 'Empathic distress fatigue rather than compassion fatigue? Integrating findings from empathy research in psychology and social neuroscience.' *Pathological Altruism,* 368–383.

21. Vreeling, K., Kersemaekers, W., Cillessen, L., van Dierendonck, D., & Speckens A. (2019). 'How medical specialists experience the effects of a mindful leadership course on their leadership capabilities: A qualitative interview study in the Netherlands'. *BMJ Open, 9*(12), e031643. doi: 10.1136/bmjopen–2019–031643.

22. Reb, J., Narayanan, J., & Chaturvedi, S. (2014). 'Leading mindfully: Two studies on the influence of supervisor trait mindfulness on employee wellbeing and performance.' *Mindfulness, 5*(1), 36–45. https://doi.org/10.1007/s12671–012–0144–z

23. Olafsen, A. H., Halvari, H., & Frølund, C. W. (2021). 'The basic psychological need satisfaction and need frustration at work scale: A validation study.' *Front Psychol., 12,* 697306. doi:10.3389/fpsyg.2021.697306.

24. Reb, J., Narayanan, J., & Ho, Z. W. (2015). 'Mindfulness at work: Antecedents and consequences of employee awareness and absent-mindedness.' *Mindfulness, 6*(1), 111–122. https://doi.org/10.1007/s12671–013–0236–4

25. Amar, A. D., Hlupic, V., & Tamwatin, T. (2014). 'Effect of meditation

on self-perception of leadership skills: A controlled group study of CEOs.' *Academy of Management Annual Meeting Proceedings, 1,* 14282. DOI:10.5465/AMBPP.2014.300

26. Arendt, J. F. W., Pircher Verdorfer, A., & Kugler, K. G. (2019). 'Mindfulness and leadership: Communication as a behavioral correlate of leader mindfulness and its effect on follower satisfaction.' *Front Psychol., 10,* 667. doi: 10.3389/fpsyg.2019.00667.

27. Glomb, T. M., Duffy, M. K., Bono, J. E., & Yang, T. (2011). 'Mindfulness at work.' In *Research in Personnel and Human Resources Management* (Vol. 30), eds A. Joshi, H. Liao & J. J. Martocchio. Emerald Group Publishing Limited, pp. 115–157. https://doi.org/10.1108/S0742–7301(2011)0000030005

28. Long, E. C., & Christian, M. S. (2015). 'Mindfulness buffers retaliatory responses to injustice: A regulatory approach.' *Journal of Applied Psychology, 100*(5), 1409–1422. https://doi.org/10.1037/apl0000019

29. Liang, L. H., Brown, D. J., Ferris, D. L., Hanig, S., Lian, H., & Keeping, L. M. (2018). 'The dimensions and mechanisms of mindfulness in regulating aggressive behaviors'. *J Appl Psychol., 103*(3), 281–299. doi: 10.1037/apl0000283.

30. Walsh, M. M., & Arnold, K. A. (2018). 'Mindfulness as a buffer of leaders' self-rated behavioral responses to emotional exhaustion: A dual process model of self-regulation.' *Front Psychol., 9,* 2498. doi:10.3389/fpsyg.2018.02498.

31. Chen, Z. (2018). 'A literature review of team-member exchange and prospects.' *Journal of Service Science and Management, 11,* 433–454. doi: 10.4236/jssm.2018.114030.

32. Hawkes, A. J., & Neale, C. M. (2020). 'Mindfulness beyond wellbeing: Emotion regulation and team-member exchange in the workplace.' *Australian Journal of Psychology, 72*(1), 20–30, DOI:10.1111/ajpy.12255

33. Yu, L., & Zellmer-Bruhn, M. (2018). 'Introducing team mindfulness and considering its safeguard role against conflict transformation and social undermining.' *Academy of Management Journal, 61*(1), 324–34. https://doi.org/10.5465/amj.2016.0094

34. Reb, J., Narayanan, J., & Chaturvedi, S. (2012). 'Leading mindfully: Two studies on the influence of supervisor trait mindfulness on employee well-being and performance.' *Mindfulness,* 1(1). doi:10.1007/s12671–012–0144–z

Chapter 5

1. https://quoteinvestigator.com/2017/10/23/be-change/#f+17089+1+1. From Lorrance, A. (1974). 'The love project.' In *Developing Priorities and a Style: Selected readings in education for teachers and parents*, ed. R. D. Kellough. MSS Information Corporation, p. 85.

2. Fahrenkopf, A. M., Sectish, T. C., Barger, L. K., Sharek, P. J., Lewin, D., Chiang, V. W., Edwards, S., Wiedermann, B. L., & Landrigan, C. P. (2008). 'Rates of medication errors among depressed and burnt-out residents: Prospective cohort study.' *BMJ (Clinical research ed.)*, 336(7642), 488–491. https://doi.org/10.1136/bmj.39469.763218.BE

3. Kim, S. E., Kim, J. W., & Jee, Y. S. (2015). 'Relationship between smartphone addiction and physical activity in Chinese international students in Korea.' *Journal of Behavioral Addictions*, 4(3), 200–205. https://doi.org/10.1556/2006.4.2015.028

4. Alshobaili, F. A., & AlYousefi, N. A. (2019). 'The effect of smartphone usage at bedtime on sleep quality among Saudi non-medical staff at King Saud University Medical City.' *Journal of Family Medicine and Primary Care*, 8(6), 1953–1957. https://doi.org/10.4103/jfmpc.jfmpc_269_19

5. Demirci, K., Akgönül, M., & Akpinar, A. (2015). 'Relationship of smartphone use severity with sleep quality, depression, and anxiety in university students.' *Journal of Behavioral Addictions*, 4(2), 85–92. https://doi.org/10.1556/2006.4.2015.010

6. Pearce, M., Garcia, L., Abbas, A., Strain, T., Schuch, F. B., Golubic, R., Kelly, P., Khan, S., Utukuri, M., Laird, Y., Mok, A., Smith, A., Tainio, M., Brage, S., & Woodcock, J. (2022). 'Association between physical activity and risk of depression: A systematic review and meta-analysis.' *JAMA Psychiatry*, 79(6), 550–559. https://doi.org/10.1001/jamapsychiatry.2022.0609

7. Rosenbaum, S., Tiedemann, A., Stanton, R., Parker, A., Waterreus, A., Curtis, J., & Ward, P. B. (2015). 'Implementing evidence-based physical activity interventions for people with mental illness: An Australian perspective.' *Australas Psychiatry*, ii. 1039856215590252.

8. Firth, J., Marx, W., Dash, S., et al. (2019). 'The effects of dietary improvement on symptoms of depression and anxiety: A meta-analysis of randomized controlled trials.' *Psychosom Med.* doi: 10.1097/PSY.0000000000000673.

9. Hobfoll, S. E. (2011). 'Conservation of resources theory: Its implication for stress, health, and resilience.' In *The Oxford Handbook of Stress,*

Health, and Coping, ed. S. Folkman. Oxford University Press, pp. 127–147.

10. Baror, S., & Bar, M. (2016). 'Associative activation and its relation to exploration and exploitation in the brain.' *Psychol Sci.*, *27*(6), 776–89. doi: 10.1177/0956797616634487.

11. Beaty, R. E., Benedek, M., Kaufman, S. B., & Silvia, P. J. (2015). 'Default and executive network coupling supports creative idea production.' *Scientific Reports*, *5*(10964). doi:10.1038/srep10964

12. https://www2.deloitte.com/us/en/insights/topics/leadership/employee–wellness–in–the–corporate–workplace.html

13. Mazmanian, M., Orlikowski, W. J., & Yates, J. (2013). 'The autonomy paradox: The implications of mobile email devices for knowledge professionals.' *Organization Science*, *24*(5), 1337–1357.

14. Lanaj, K., Johnson, R. E., & Barnes, C. M. (2014). 'Beginning the workday yet already depleted? Consequences of late-night smartphone use and sleep.' *Organizational Behavior and Human Decision Processes*, *124*(1), 11–23.

15. Derks, D., Bakker, A. B., Peters, P., & van Wingerden, P. (2016). 'Work-related smartphone use, work–family conflict and family role performance: The role of segmentation preference.' *Human Relations*, *69*(5), 1045–1068.

16. Steffensen, D. S., McAllister, C. P., Perrewé, P. L., Wang, G., & Brooks, C. D. (2022). '"You've got mail": A daily investigation of email demands on job tension and work–family conflict.' *Journal of Business and Psychology,* *37*(2), 325–338.

17. Derks, D., Bakker, A. B., Peters, P., & van Wingerden, P. (2016). 'Work-related smartphone use, work–family conflict and family role performance: The role of segmentation preference.' *Human Relations*, *69*(5), 1045–1068.

18. Singh, P., Bala, H., Lal Dey, B., & Filieri, R. (2022). 'Enforced remote working: The impact of digital platform-induced stress and remote working experience on technology exhaustion and subjective wellbeing.' *Journal of Business Research*, *151*, 269–286. ISSN 0148–2963, https://doi.org/10.1016/j.jbusres.2022.07.002

19. Xiao, Y., Becerik-Gerber, B., Lucas, G., & Roll, S. C. (2021). 'Impacts of working from home during COVID-19 pandemic on physical and mental well-being of office workstation users.' *J Occup Environ Med*, *63*(3), 181–190. doi: 10.1097/JOM.0000000000002097.

20. Galanti, T., Guidetti, G., Mazzei, E., Zappalà, S., & Toscano, F. (2021). 'Work from home during the COVID-19 outbreak: The impact on

employees' remote work productivity, engagement, and stress.' *J Occup Environ Med, 63*(7), e426–e432. doi: 10.1097/JOM.0000000000002236.

21. Chu, A. M. Y., Chan, T. W. C., & So, M. K. P. (2022). 'Learning from work-from-home issues during the COVID-19 pandemic: Balance speaks louder than words.' *PLoS One, 17*(1), e0261969. doi:10.1371/journal.pone.0261969.

22. Tejero, L. M. S., Seva, R. R., & Fadrilan-Camacho, V. F. F. (2021). 'Factors associated with work–life balance and productivity before and during work from home.' *J Occup Environ Med, 63*(12), 1065–1072. doi: 10.1097/JOM.0000000000002377.

23. Stothart, C., Mitchum, A., & Yehnert, C. (2015). 'The attentional cost of receiving a cell phone notification.' *Journal of Experimental Psychology. Human Perception and Performance, 41*(4), 893–897. https://doi.org/10.1037/xhp0000100

24. Jackson, T., Dawson, R., & Wilson, D. (2001). 'The cost of email interruption.' *Journal of Systems and Information Technology, 5*(1), 81–92. https://doi.org/10.1108/13287260180000760

25. Puranik, H., Koopman, J., & Vough, H. C. (2021). 'Excuse me, do you have a minute? An exploration of the dark- and bright-side effects of daily work interruptions for employee well-being.' *Journal of Applied Psychology, 106*(12), 1867–1884.

26. Lin, L. Y., Sidani, J. E., Shensa, A., et al. (2016). 'Association between social media use and depression among U.S. young adults.' *Depress Anxiety, 33*(4), 323–31. doi: 10.1002/da.22466.

27. Reed, P., Bircek, N. I., Osborne, L. A., Viganò, C., & Truzoli, R. (2018). 'Visual social media use moderates the relationship between initial problematic Internet use and later narcissism.' *Open Psychology Journal, 11*(1), 163. DOI:10.2174/1874350101811010163

28. Clark, J. L., Algoe, S. B., Green, M. C., et al. (2017). 'Social network sites and well-being: The role of social connection.' *Current Directions in Psychological Science.* https://doi.org/10.1177/0963721417730833

29. Reb, J., Narayanan, J., & Chaturvedi, S. (2012). 'Leading mindfully: Two studies on the influence of supervisor trait mindfulness on employee well-being and performance.' *Mindfulness, 1*(1). doi:10.1007/s12671-012-0144-z

Chapter 7

1. In one version of the myth, Medusa was a virgin in the temple of Athena, the goddess of wisdom, and was ravished by Poseidon on the

steps of Athena's temple. Athena then banished Medusa to the isle of Sarpedon and cursed her. As part of the curse, she grew hair made of snakes and her stare turned any recipient to stone.

2. Simonsson, O., Bazin, O., Fisher, S. D., & Goldberg, S. B. (2022). 'Effects of an 8-week mindfulness course on affective polarization'. *Mindfulness, 13*(2), 474–483. https://doi.org/10.1007/s12671–021–01808–0

3. Simonsson, O., Goldberg, S. B., Marks, J., Yan, L., & Narayanan, J. (2022). 'Bridging the (Brexit) divide: Effects of a brief befriending meditation on affective polarization.' *PloS one, 17*(5), e0267493. https://doi.org/10.1371/journal.pone.0267493

4. Newport, C. (2019). *Digital Minimalism: On living better with less technology*. Portfolio/Penguin.

5. Radtke, T., Apel, T., Schenkel, K., Keller, J., & von Lindern, E. (2022). 'Digital detox: An effective solution in the smartphone era? A systematic literature review.' *Mobile Media & Communication, 10*(2), 190–215. https://doi.org/10.1177/20501579211028647

6. Kang, C. (2023). 'OpenAI 's Sam Altman urges AI regulation hearing.' *The New York Times.* https://www.nytimes.com/2023/05/16/technology/openai-altman-artificial-intelligence-regulation.html

7. Unesco. (2023). https://www.unesco.org/en/artificial-intelligence/recommendation-ethics

8. Autor, D., Mindell, D. A., & Reynolds, E. B. (2022). *Why the Future of AI is the Future of Work*. MIT Management Sloan School. https://mitsloan.mit.edu/ideas–made–to–matter/why–future–ai–future–work

9. Ibid.

10. Relihan, T. (2019). *A Calm Before the AI Productivity Storm*. MIT Management Sloan School. https://mitsloan.mit.edu/ideas–made–to–matter/a–calm–ai–productivity–storm

11. Naylor, M., Ridout, B., & Campbell, A. (2020). 'A scoping review identifying the need for quality research on the use of virtual reality in workplace settings for stress management.' *Cyberpsychology, Behavior, and Social Networking, 23*(8). https://doi.org/10.1089/cyber.2019.0287

12. Naylor, M., Morrison, B., Ridout, B., & Campbell, A. (2019). 'Augmented experiences: Investigating the feasibility of virtual reality as part of a workplace wellbeing intervention.' *Interacting with Computers, 31*(5), 507–523. https://doi.org/10.1093/iwc/iwz033

13. Hawkins, M. (2022). 'Virtual employee training and skill development, workplace technologies, and deep learning computer vision algorithms

in the immersive metaverse environment.' *Psychosociological Issues in Human Resource Management*, 10(1), 106–120. DOI:10.22381/pihrm10120228

14. Michalos, G., Karvouniari, A., Dimitropoulos, N., Togias, T., & Makris, S. (2018). 'Workplace analysis and design using virtual reality techniques.' *CIRP Annals, 67*(1), 141–144. https://doi.org/10.1016/j.cirp.2018.04.120.

15. Caputo, F., Greco, A., D'Amato, E., Notaro, I., & Spada, S. (2018). 'On the use of Virtual Reality for a human-centered workplace design.' *Procedia Structural Integrity, 8*, 297–308. https://doi.org/10.1016/j.prostr.2017.12.031.

16. Simonetto, M., Arena, S., & Peron, M. (2022). 'A methodological framework to integrate motion capture system and virtual reality for assembly system 4.0 workplace design.' *Safety Science, 146*, https://doi.org/10.1016/j.ssci.2021.105561

17. Souchet, A. D., Lourdeaux, D., Pagani, A., et al. (2022). 'A narrative review of immersive virtual reality's ergonomics and risks at the workplace: cybersickness, visual fatigue, muscular fatigue, acute stress, and mental overload.' *Virtual Reality.* https://doi.org/10.1007/s10055-022-00672-0

18. Aardema, F., O'Connor, K., Côté, S., & Taillon, A. (2010). 'Virtual reality induces dissociation and lowers sense of presence in objective reality.' *Cyberpsychology, Behavior and Social Networking, 13*(4), 429–435. https://doi.org/10.1089/cyber.2009.0164

19. Peckmann, C., Kannen, K., Pensel, M. C., Lux, S., Philipsen, A., & Braun, N. (2022). 'Virtual reality induces symptoms of depersonalization and derealization: A longitudinal randomised control trial.' *Computers in Human Behavior, 131*(C). https://doi.org/10.1016/j.chb.2022.107233

20. Barreda-Ángeles, M., & Hartmann, T. (2022). 'Hooked on the metaverse? Exploring the prevalence of addiction to virtual reality applications.' *Frontiers in Virtual Reality, 3*, 1–9. [1031697]. https://doi.org/10.3389/frvir.2022.1031697

Index

the bullseye 191, 219
clear sense of 54–5
communicating 59–60
consistently embodied 60–2
different courses of action 65–7
engaging team around 56–7
finding team's 43–5
keeping fresh and tangible 58–9
leading with 50–67
between motivational drivers 49
needs clear sense of why 55
policy recommendations 74–5
statement of 48, 51–8
team statement 44
used to navigate complexity 63–5

Q

questions, art of asking 135–7

R

Ravi, son asks what father does at work
78–9
'reality', less able to distinguish 212
reliability, keeping your word 68–9
resolution
by communication 13–14
Cuban missile crisis 15–16
road accidents, misuse of technology 84
robots, human needs 212
rocks in the jar metaphor 157–8, 183,
185
role-modelling, by leaders 61–2
Roosevelt, Eleanor 125
Rosling, Hans 97
Rumelt, Richard 87–8

S

Schein, Edgar 55
self-awareness, creating greater 136
self-care
effective leaders 127
focus on own 158
importance of 156
not selfish 154–8
setting boundaries 153–4

taking time for 161–2
self-image 179
self-medication 160
self-renewal, making time for 182
self-replenishment 159–62
simple moments, keeping simple 87
Slack messages, volume of 26, 78–9
sleep
irregular pattern 160
rules for device use 175
SMART actions 202
SMART goal, implementing 161–2
smartphones
addiction to 35–6
dependence on 30–1
impact of 132
reduction in performance 84
sense of connectedness 35
see also devices
social cognition, explained 133
social impact, always-on culture 35–6
social media
focus on self 179
impact on mental health 179
impacts of 178–80
leaders use of 180
weaponized 19
startup business team, transitional
growth 52–3
statistics
changing jobs 169
compulsive VR use 215
open-plan office communications 25
productivity hours lost 176–7
smartphone dependence 30–1
text message interruption error rate
176
strategic challenges, approach to 88
strategic decisions 59
strategic leadership, self-assessment 89
stress
automatic pilot reactions 126
effect on performance 168
stress management, conservation of
resources theory 161
sunk-cost bias 106
switching off, encouraging 115